Teaching... Take

Teaching . . .
Take This Job and Love It!

Jerry King

Insight Publishing Company
Sevierville, TN

Teaching... Take This Job and Love It!

For information contact: Insight Publishing Company, Inc., 134 Court Ave., Ste. 108, Sevierville, TN, 37864, 1-865-429-0252.

Published in Sevierville, Tennessee, by Insight Publishing Company, Inc.

First Printing 2001
ISBN No. 1-885640-77-3
Library of congress cataloging-in-Publication data

Dedication

This book is dedicated to:

My wife, Lucy: This book - and my life - would be impossible without your unfailing love, patience, support, and faith in me. You 'teach' me what is truly important in life...unconditional loving relationships!

My sons, Jon and Chris: I am so proud of what you guys have become, who you are, and your unlimited potential in the future. You 'teach' me not to sweat the small stuff in life and to have fun - even at my old age!

This book is in memory of:
My sister, Ronda King, whose courageous fight with Lupus, and my mother, Stella King, whose hard-fought battle with cancer, ended in victory. You both 'taught' me that laughter really is the best medicine during life's difficult times and that living a life of significance is more important than any "success" on earth!

Thanks!

I sincerely appreciate each person who contributed, directly or indirectly, to the completion of one of my biggest goals and dreams...writing a book to help teachers achieve success in their personal and professional life!

Thanks to every person whose research, work or publication was used as a resource.

Thanks to the wonderful people at Insight Publishing Company. A special "thank you" to David Wright, President, for his professional and personal assistance from the beginning to the end of this project. Also, to Sandy Sullivan for her hard work and long hours in editing the manuscript.

Thanks to Sandy Worrell for her outstanding photography expertise used for the cover. Also, to Douglas Graphics for the cover design.

Thanks to God, my Creator, for giving me the opportunity to learn from so many dedicated "teachers" from all walks of life!

To All School Teachers

YOU are the most influential people in the world!
YOU are the true "heroes" of our time!
YOU make a positive difference in the lives
of young people every day!
YOU plant the seeds of greatness that mold lives.

I hope the information in this book will help you continue the positive, life changing job you do and lead you further on life's exciting journey of success for yourself, your family and your students.
God bless you!

"Teaching . . . Take This Job and Love It!"
The 6 Dynamic Strategies of Highly Successful Teachers

Table of Contents

Stage I

Stage II

Stage III

**"My father and mother wanted me to be a brain surgeon, but I exceeded all their expectations . . .
I BECAME A TEACHER!"**

Harry K. Wong

**The mediocre teacher tells.
The good teacher explains.
The superior teacher demonstrates.
The great teacher inspires.**

William Arthur Ward

A New Day for Teachers!

This is the beginning of a new day! God has given me this day to use as I will. I'm a teacher, motivator of learning and builder of foundations. I can waste today or use it for good. I can go to school prepared and enthusiastic or grumble about my job and its many responsibilities. I can look at it as a challenge to grow or just another long day to get through.

What I do today is important, because I am exchanging one day of my life for it. I can never go back and re-do it . . . so I have to get it right the first time – to understand sympathetically, to listen sincerely, to share openly, to teach creatively . . . to do my best!

When tomorrow comes, this day will be gone forever, leaving in its place something that I have traded for it. It was my decision and my choice that shaped my attitude and actions today. I want this day to be a gain, not loss; good, not evil; success, not failure; in order that I shall not regret the high price I paid for today.

I want to say at the end of today, "I succeeded in reaching my students; I showed an earnest concern for others and I helped my class grow in knowledge and self-esteem."

I paid one whole day of my life and I need to know it was worthwhile; it counted for something special. It was a good day and tomorrow can even be better!!

Adapted by Lana Eckard

> "Most of us end up with no more than five or six people who remember us. Teachers have thousands of people who remember them for the rest of their lives."
> Andy Rooney, Journalist

Teacher Success Strategy # 1

Unleash Your Personal Power With a Dynamic Self-Image!

YOU! Yes -YOU. . . are a unique, one-of-a-kind person who was born to be a winner - in the classroom and in life! You have unlimited potential to become the person you were meant to be! The fact that you opened this book and are reading these words is evidence that you want more out of life than you are currently getting. You have taken the first and most important step toward *making your dreams become a reality!*

As a teacher, you are experiencing unprecedented stress and responsibilities and a weekly grinding routine that probably includes:

faculty meetings, parent-teacher meetings, preparing and grading tests, bus duty/cafeteria duty/game duty, committee meetings, preparing lesson plans, in-service meetings, averaging grades . . .and did I mention - *more meetings*?

If you are like thousands of other teachers, many nights you turn the light off, pull the covers up to your chin, exhale with a big sigh and think, "Is this it? Is this what teaching, (and life), are all about?" If you feel like you are on the "treadmill of life" and don't know how to get off, this book was written for *you*! If you feel overworked, underpaid, unappreciated and unfulfilled in your personal and professional life, this book was written for *you.* And if you are experiencing a mountaintop "high" in your life, this book is also for you. You will be able to get even *more* out of life.

How optimistic about your future are you? Have your dreams become a reality? One of the saddest situations in life is when our dreams become regrets. Regardless of your current situation at school and home, remember:

**When your dreams are big enough,
the facts don't count!**

Each of us has dreams. As teachers, we all want to believe that we have a special gift and can make a difference in young people's lives. We all want to touch others in a special way. In fact, at one time in our lives we could "see" ourselves experiencing a high quality of life.

Yet, for many of us those dreams have become as blurred as wearing out-of-focus glasses or dirty contact lenses. Our frustrations and routines of daily life - at school and home - have resulted in no longer even *trying* to accomplish the things we dreamed of at the beginning of our teaching career.

I have great news for you! There **is** more to life - without changing jobs! There **is** hope for you to live the fulfilling life you were created to live! **There is hope for YOU!**

"When there is hope for the future,
there is power in the present."
Dr. John C. Maxwell

Susan was born in severe poverty and was too embarrassed to go to elementary school because she only had one dress - but *she had big dreams and hope*. She earned her PhD. in education and became a leading university professor.

Jim was so obese, he had to lose over 170 pounds before he could buckle the seatbelt in his car. He hated every minute of every day as a teacher - but *he had big dreams and hope*. After losing his weight, he started a wellness and exercise class for teachers at his school. Because of his newly found self-confidence, two years later was recognized for his enthusiasm and love for children as he was named "Teacher of the Year."

As a child, Juanita was physically and sexually abused so horribly that she dropped out of high school. She swore she could never trust anyone enough to have a loving relationship with them *She also had big dreams and hope.* She eventually received her high school and college diploma, married the "relationship of my dreams," and later started a school-counseling program, which has become a tremendous success!

Just like these people and thousands of others, **YOU** have within you the same **Personal Power**. Personal Power simply means you have the ability to **take action!**

Research of the 100 most successful people in the world revealed that 70% of them had to overcome poverty, abuse, or a physical handicap. These people attributed their success to the fact that they became successful *because* of the challenges they had to conquer.

What challenges do you have to conquer in your classroom, and more importantly - in your life?

Do you have a success plan for your personal and professional life? This handbook for teachers is *your* blueprint for success!

If <u>you</u> don't have a plan for your life,
someone else does.

Think of a movie you liked so much you watched it more than one time. Now a question with an obvious, but profound answer. Each time you watched the movie, did it end the same way? Of course it did. Most teachers want different results, (a different ending), but think they can keep doing the same thing. **You must <u>change</u> your thoughts, beliefs and actions if you want different results**. (Griping about situations in your personal life or about your job as a teacher won't bring different results. It takes a positive plan of action.)

**If you keep doin' what you've been doin',
you're gonna keep getting' what you've got!**

This book includes a proven success plan for YOU! If there are areas of your life you are not satisfied with, you must ***change*** your game plan. This book will help you get the results you want!

Have you looked at your high school yearbook lately? Any doubts you may have about how much we have changed will quickly vanish by taking a few quick glances at yourself and members of your senior class. (Nice haircut - and how about those clothes?)

Remember the Hoolahoop, Slinky, and Silly Putty? Even though they are still sold in stores, they are not nearly the "hot item" today. Why? Times, people, needs and wants *change*.

Need proof that schools have changed and "just ain't what they used to be?" Read the following list of teacher responsibilities in 1915:

Rules of Conduct for Teachers

(Board of Education School Bulletin, 1915)

1. You will not marry during the terms of your contract.

2. You are not to keep company with men.

3. You must be home between the hours of 8:00 p.m. and 6:00 a.m. unless attending a school function.

4. You may not loiter in downtown ice cream stores.

5. You may not travel beyond city limits unless you have permission of the chairman of the board.

6. You may not ride in a carriage or automobile with any man, unless he is your father or brother.

7. You may not smoke cigarettes.

8. You may not dress in bright colors.

9. You may under no circumstances dye your hair.

10. You must wear at least two petticoats.

11. Your dresses must not be any shorter than two inches above your ankles.

12. To keep the schoolroom neat and clean, you must sweep the floor at least once a week with hot, soapy water; clean the blackboards at least once a day; and start the fire by 7:00 a.m. so the room will be warm by 8:00 a.m.

During my elementary school years I lived in South Carolina. I remember how hot the pavement felt when I ran barefooted across it during those scorching summers. I screamed as the bottom of my feet touched the sizzling asphalt. Like running across those roads, **making changes in our lives may sometimes bring temporary discomfort and pain**. But highly successful teachers aren't satisfied to "stand in the middle" of mediocrity and just be "average."

> "Education is a wonderful thing. If you couldn't sign your name you'd have to pay cash."
> Rita Mae Brown

To get more out of your life, you must be willing to take risks and break out of your comfort zone with every ounce of energy you have. If you wait until every situation is "right," you will probably wait forever.

Be aware of the three things keeping you from breaking out of your "circle of sameness" and from experiencing the happiness you were meant to enjoy. The **FUD Factor** consists of **F**ear, **U**ncertainty and **D**oubt. All of us have them. For example, I'm not particularly fond of riding roller coasters. What's one of your fears? Don't allow your FUD's to keep you from becoming the highly successful teacher and person you can be!

***Important Questions**:* **What if you knew you only had one day - tomorrow - left to live?**
Would you do anything differently? Who are the people you would visit or call? Are there people you would spend more time with? Let's apply the same thought-line to your profession as a teacher: If you *had* to teach tomorrow - your last day on earth - what would you do differently? Would you treat everyone at school the same as usual - students, teachers, administrators, staff - as if it were "just another day?" What kind of teacher would you want them to remember you?

If you think there are some people and situations you would handle differently, then why not begin *changing* and doing some of those things today . . . **right now?** Don't put off beginning your journey of success. *Procrastination is one of the leading killers of success!*

A painfully shy man fell deeply in love with a young woman. He sensed that she felt the same way, but he couldn't find the courage to ask her out. Finally he decided he would mail her a love letter every day for one year, and then ask her out for a date.

Faithfully, he followed his plan, and at the end of the year he was courageous enough to call her - only to find out she had married the mailman! Don't procrastinate!

Live and teach every day of your life as if it were your last, because one day you will be exactly right!

To benefit most from this book, you will need to do more than just *read* it. I will ask you to "*do*" this book. (Please use a highlighter and pen to "do" this teacher handbook and mark important points, quotes, etc. and complete the Success Activities.) Your new journey of success begins with your honest, personal affirmation of your decision to *change* and get more out of life than you are currently getting. I refer to these as the **"3 Gottas":** (Please rewrite each statement on the line following it to affirm your decision to change.)

"I gotta . . . be open to new possibilities!"

____

"I gotta . . . be committed to action!"

____

"I gotta . . . bust out of my comfort zone!"

____

(My apology if you are an English teacher. I am well aware "gotta" is slang and the word *burst* is more appropriate than *bust*, but I will take advantage of writer's freedom. Also, I write on the seventh grade, third month level . . . so school administrators and college professors can understand what I am trying to say. Just kidding! I am appreciative and thankful for the sense of humor school administrators have - especially those in the school divisions in which I have had the privilege to teach.)

The following story is one of my favorites. A school administrator shared it with me:

A man in a hot air balloon realized he was lost. He reduced altitude and spotted a woman below. He descended a bit more and shouted, "Excuse me, can you help me? I promised a friend I would meet him an hour ago, but I don't know where I am."

The woman replied, "You are in a hot air balloon hovering about 30 feet above the ground, between 40 and 41 degrees north latitude, and between 59 and 60 degrees west longitude."
"You must be a teacher," said the balloonist. "I am" replied the

woman, "but how did you know?"

"Well" answered the man, "everything you told me is technically correct, but I have no idea what to make of your information, and the fact is, I am still lost. Frankly, you haven't been much help to me so far."

The teacher responded, "You must be a school administrator." "I am," replied the balloonist, but how did you know that?" "Well" said the woman, "You don't know where you are or where you are going. You have risen to where you are due to a lot of hot air. You made a promise which you have no idea how to keep, and you expect ME to solve your problem. The fact is, sir, you're in exactly the same position you were in before we met, but now, somehow it's MY fault!"

✎"Teachers are real people, too - almost."✎

During my first year of teaching one of my students saw me pushing my cart through the grocery store. After quickly scanning the contents of my cart, full of the usual junk food items of my typical shopping spree - Dr. Pepper, doughnuts, chips and dip and three ½ gallons of ice cream - she exclaimed, "Wow, Mr. King, I guess teachers are real people, too - almost." As a teacher, standing in front of your class, did it ever occur to you that many of your students don't even consider you a *real human being*?

As a speaker and presenter at many educator conferences and in-service training programs throughout the country, I have observed very few, if any, that address the strategies and importance of teachers experiencing a successful *personal life*. As a teacher, you will only be successful *in* the classroom if you are experiencing success *outside* the classroom.

As often as educators may try to separate the two: it's impossible to do. I've read the same books you have, telling us to leave our personal problems at home. That's one of those concepts that "looks good on paper," but in the real world of teaching - just doesn't work. If you are extremely stressed out about a relationship or situation in your personal life, can it affect your performance in the classroom? Of course it can, and *will* control you, *if you* allow it to. (Strategy #3 for Highly Successful Teachers specifically deals with how you can successfully manage teacher stress and burnout. The success strategies are to be learned in the order given, so try to resist the temptation to skip to #3.)

This is the reason the first three strategies directly pertain to your personal life. To include only "classroom strategies" would be unfair to you and your students. For you to be successful at school, you must first be successful in your personal life - beginning with improving your "self-image."

Successful *people* become successful *teachers*!

This book has absolutely no value whatsoever to help you in life, unless you *apply* the strategies you read. Even the number one success book in the world, the Holy Bible, (which I *highly* recommend), will not change you until you *practice* its powerful success principles.

"Halloween is over. You can take your mask off."

How many times have you heard those statements from students the day after Halloween? (Actually, they say it to me all year.) These success strategies will make a positive difference in your life only to the extent you *apply them* and are honest with yourself. This is not Halloween. No masks allowed. You are not trying to fool anyone. You will discover that the truth about yourself will give you more energy and enthusiasm than you can imagine possible - both in the classroom and at home!

The age-old wisdom, "*You will reap what you sow*" is still true. **Sow a seed, reap a reward**.

Sew apathy in the classroom - Reap students who don't care about school or your class
Sew disorganization and no preparation - Reap classroom discipline problems
Sew disrespect and impatience at home - Reap broken relationships

Sew enthusiasm in the classroom - Reap motivated students who complete their assignments
Sew preparation - Reap students who don't have time to become discipline problems
Sew love and patience at home - Reap more loving, lasting personal relationships

Are you satisfied with what you are reaping? If not, I encourage you to *change* what you are sewing . . . beginning right now! Remember:

In order to *have* the things you want, you must *be* the right kind of person and *do* the right things. Follow these proven teacher success strategies and you will reap a positive, fulfilling life you never thought possible!

You must answer the same question coaches asks their team during half time of a close game. **How badly do you want it?**

You must want it badly enough to apply these success strategies and make a commitment to doing them every day. Some teachers are willing to make a little sacrifice, but to really make a positive difference in your life; **you must make a total 100% commitment!** I challenge anyone to convince a couple that has been married for 20+ years, to say their relationship worked because they both put forth a 50% effort. Both people had to make a 100% commitment - not 50/50!

There is a big difference between commitment and sacrifice. A great example is the farmer who sat down to eat breakfast, and looking at his plate of ham and eggs said, "The chicken made a sacrifice, but the hog made a total commitment!" (You won't need to give your life for success, but you must be willing to make changes necessary to get the results you want.)

Remember, if you want different results in your personal and professional life, you must decide to *do* something different - not just *read* about it in this book.

No excuses accepted-even those signed by your parents! Ever seen that school policy? If you truly decide to do something and follow through with it, you can accomplish almost anything!

You must make a decision - today - right now! From this point, decide you will **not** accept a life of mediocrity! Wherever you are in life, (just beginning teaching or retiring next month), or whatever situations you may be experiencing (struggling with personal or professional relationships, or possibly dealing with health problems), you must stick to your decision that, by using the success strategies in this book, **you will find a way!**

Successful people are willing to break out of a life of comfort and live a life of commitment!

I wrote this book because, as a teacher, I want you to experience an exciting wake-up-call that will make a dramatic, positive difference in your life! I challenge you to make a decision and commit yourself to become the winner in your personal and professional life you were born to be! I want you to get everything out of life you can . . . beginning NOW!

I sincerely believe in you as a person and as a teacher. I believe that no matter how impossible you think some situations seem right now, you can come out on top! I believe you are destined to become your own unique form of greatness. Not someone else . . . YOUR form of greatness! *Your decision to practice these success strategies can literally change your life!*

"It is in your moments of decision that your destiny is shaped."
Anthony Robbins

The 6 Dynamic Strategies of Highly Successful Teachers can get you out of the rut of life we all experience at one time or another. Someone asked me what the difference between a rut and a grave was and I said, "About 6 inches!" Living our lives in a humdrum *rut* keeps us from enjoying life and loving the people we care about most.

Whenever I think of a *rut*, I remember my grandfather, who was a farmer and owner of a sawmill. When the huge logging trucks went up the mountain after a heavy rain, they would leave big ruts in the logging road. My grandfather, who had a great sense of humor, placed a sign at the bottom of the mountain, which read, **"Please choose your rut wisely - You will be in it for 2 miles."** If you don't make changes, you may be like thousands of other teachers who have only *survived* life in a rut, but not really *lived life*!

> "If you promise not to believe everything your child says happens at school, I promise not to believe everything she/he says happened at home." Teacher at Parents Meeting

I ask you to make a commitment to not only read these dynamic strategies for success, but to make such a total personal commitment you need to *sign you name*. What is so special about signing your name?

Everything significant in your life required a signature. Think about it. Before you were released from the hospital at birth, someone signed his or her name. When you graduated from high school or college, someone signed his or her name. If you are married, someone signed his or her name. When you made a major purchase or bank loan, you signed your name. **Your signature is special because it means you are someone special and you will do what you agree to do!**

IMPORTANT: By signing the **"*Teacher Success Commitment Pledge*"** below, you understand that when you *read and apply* the success strategies in this book, you will experience dramatic positive changes in your life - some of them beginning immediately!

Teacher Success Commitment Pledge

I want to improve my personal and professional life and begin a new journey of success. I want to make my dreams a reality and become the winner in life I was born to be. I realize this requires commitment, change, and honesty with myself. I will read this book in its entirety and complete every exercise and activity. I will apply *all* 6 Dynamic Strategies of Highly Successful Teachers and practice the *"10-Day Personal and Professional Power Plan."* Knowing with confidence that in doing so . . .

I WILL BECOME HIGHLY SUCCESSFUL!!

____

Signature

____

Date

Congratulations on taking the first step out of your comfort zone and committing yourself to the most exciting journey of success you have ever experienced. When you take responsibility for your life and stop blaming others, it is a giant step on your success journey!

I don't know about you, but I enjoy eating good food. I especially like buffets because I can "pick and choose" all my favorites, (which usually include mostly desserts - which I don't need - and very few vegetables - which I really do need).

This book is *not* an "all you can eat" buffet.
In order for these success strategies to work in your life, You cannot choose extra helpings of the ones you like, and omit the ones you don't feel comfortable with. Read and do all 6 Dynamic Strategies of Highly Successful Teachers *in the order they are given* and they will make a profound difference in your personal and professional life!

Reminder: Reading and acquiring knowledge about your success will not bring the results in life you desire. *Doing* the right things the right way on a regular basis will help you form positive daily habits. Then you will begin to experience the happy and exciting life you were meant to have! "Just Do It!" In addition to using your highlighter and pen to complete the Success Activities and mark special thoughts, write super-special quotes or statements on blank index cards for future reference. (The more times you write it, the longer you will remember it.)

The Most Important Person in Your Success Journey

Success is not a destination, but a journey. Up to this point in your life success has depended on one person. There is one person on this earth who will decide whether you live a life of "significance or sameness." There is only one person who has the ability to make the choice of whether you will "wallow in the mire of mediocrity" and be like thousands of *average* teachers, or begin *right now* to experience a life of "excitement and meaningfulness."

That one person is . . . YOU! Not your spouse, children, or friends. Not your students, principal, or school superintendent . . . YOU! You are responsible for, and can change the direction of your life to one of success and significance.

Regardless of what you may have heard, life is not a roll of the dice where some people get lucky and "hit the jackpot." We're not talking about winning the lottery. We're talking about developing a plan that will guarantee you *real* success and significance. Ninety-nine percent of the time, people don't make more money and have better personal relationships because they are "lucky." They made many choices along the way. You also made choices that have resulted in you being exactly where you are in life today. Choices about the college you attended, your friends, spouse, and even the school where you are employed.

The Most Important Factor in Your Success Journey

The first and most important factor of your success journey is **improving the mental picture you have of yourself**. Read that statement again. (If you haven't used your highlighter, this would be a great place to begin. In fact, take a moment and highlight some of the success principles or quotes you liked up to this point.)

Your self-image will decide whether you stay in your *comfort zone* or if you have the confidence and courage to step out of your *circle of sameness* and begin to experience a new and exciting life!

Many psychologists report that every person has several areas of his/her life they lack confidence in. Areas they don't "see" themselves being successful. As a student, one of mine was standing in front of the class giving an oral book report. (Of course I would probably have felt more comfortable if I had actually read the book.) As I reflect on this experience, it's interesting to me that I - the same person who dreaded speaking to 25-30 people - now make my living speaking to hundreds of people, loving every minute of it! Simply a result of the confidence and belief that came from improving my own *self-image*.

While I attended college I worked at a fast-food restaurant. As a result of an "all-the-food-you-can-eat policy," I gained about 40 pounds and looked like Humpty Dumpty when my wife and I got married two years later. I tried every diet imaginable. I dieted religiously - which means I stopped eating while I was in church. I only lost the weight when I began to "see" myself mentally as being thinner and did the things necessary to keep it off. When my self-image improved, my health and life improved.

Teachers often ask, "How can I stay motivated while working with such negative students and peers, and living in such a negative home environment?" The solution is not easy, but is simple: **All motivation begins with a positive, successful self-image!** You will discover later in this handbook how to motivate others. But it begins with motivating yourself by improving your self-image - the picture you have placed in your mind, of who you really are.

Changing your self-image really means changing your own mental picture of yourself. Your self-image is revealed in your actions and behavior. It cannot be hidden.

Your positive self-image is a strong belief you deserve to be successful and a belief you really can do it. Most of the time we tend to focus on the negative things, which paints a negative self-picture.

For example, if your principal called you in his/her office tomorrow and said several positive things about the great job you are doing, but ended the conversation by adding, "But there is just one thing I need to mention: your lesson plan book really could be a little neater." For the rest of your day at school, would you have a tendency to think about the positive things or the one constructive criticism at the end of the conversation? Most people agree we tend to think about the negative things more than the positive.
Focus on the positive!!

List 4 positive things about yourself - 2 personal and 2 professional:

1. ______________________________
2. ______________________________
3. ______________________________
4. ______________________________

Improving your self-image by changing your habits go hand-in hand. Change one and you will automatically change the other. Ninety-five percent of our behavior is based on *habits - our automatic responses and reactions*. You must have the courage to take different action and look forward to making some mistakes. That's right - *look forward to making some mistakes.* Your journey of success will go much faster when you realize you will learn much more from mistakes and failures than your successes.

Take a moment and honestly answer the questions, "Am I excited about the direction I am going in life?" and "Exactly how and where do I see myself one year, five years or ten years from now?" **Your life was meant to be enjoyed and lived NOW - not *after* retirement!**

As I meet educators I hear their concerns about the necessity of improving the self-esteem of students. Many times we omit the importance of raising our own self-esteem by improving our own self-image.

Self-Esteem literally means *to appreciate the worth of.* A great way to appreciate the worth of ourselves is to first appreciate and respect the worth of others. Everyone has something to bring to the table: that's right - *everyone*.

Have patience with all things but first with yourself. Never confuse your mistakes with your value as a human being. You're a perfectly valuable, creative, worthwhile person simply because you exist. And no amount of triumph or tribulations can ever change that. *Unconditional self-acceptance* is the core of a peaceful mind.

St. Francis de Sales

Every fall our church celebrates a special day called Homecoming. It involves two special events: usually a guest speaker for the morning worship service and after the service a "covered dish meal." This means everyone brings a dish and "donates it for the *cause*" - *cause* we're hungry."

But something special happens. No one tells people what specific dish to bring. Some bring a casserole, some bring a dessert, and some bring a salad. But when all the dishes are placed together on the long tables, it always works out just right. You see - *everyone has something to bring to the table*!

It's the same with the students in your class, members of your faculty or family. Each person has something positive to contribute. **Look for it and you will find it**. Ever notice how you see about 10 cars exactly like the one you just bought? They didn't buy their car the same day you did. You see them because now that you own one, you begin looking for them. They were there all the time. To benefit from these teacher success strategies, remember:

"In life, you will find exactly what you look for."

Look for something in each chapter of this book to help you become a better person and a more successful teacher and YOU WILL FIND IT!

You don't ever have to worry about impressing other people because **you have value in being yourself**. Self-worth is quite different from self-conceit. I see professional athletes telling young people, by their inappropriate actions and words, how great they are. This is not self-worth, but an inflated, out-of-control ego. Genuine self-worth comes from feeling comfortable with who you are - *in private*.

It also comes from the quality of relationships that exist between a person and those who play a significant role in her/his life. Sadly, we sometimes listen to people who haven't played a positive role for us and allow them to form our self-image. If the significant people in your life have helped you paint a negative self-picture, you need to focus on the people who have painted a more positive one.

Write the name of one person who has contributed, even if in a small way, to your self-image.

____

Can you think of something they specifically did or said that helped enhance your self-picture of who you are? Something that encouraged you or made you feel more confident in yourself?

Think about how much better it made you feel. Make a daily commitment to do the same for someone else. Every day pledge to do *one small act of kindness for someone* - without expecting a "thank you" in return. Beginning today, who will it be?

"Change the *I can'ts* to *I can's*"

When I was in the first grade my parents told my teacher, "Jerry is not going to do well in math because both of us had trouble in math when we went to school." Would you guess what subject I had trouble in? You're correct - math. (Actually, I also struggled with science, English, social studies . . . but, as they say, that's another story.)

> "Teaching provides a way to stay young at heart, to maintain a lifetime of active learning. It is in every aspect a profession of hope." Vito Perrone, American teacher

I asked you earlier to be honest with yourself while you read and *do* this book. I will also be honest and tell you that later in life I "woke up" to the importance of an education, and eventually received my graduate degree from Virginia Tech. But during elementary and part of high school I had to show my parents a lot of report cards that read - let's see, how did the teacher word it . . . "Jerry is not working up to his (what's the word) potential!" (If you thought of the word before I did, I guess that means you had the same thing written your report card, right? You're in good company.)

If you are an educator who excelled in the classroom for 12 years and maintained a GPA of 4.0 my hat goes off to you. But, I find it humorous when teachers, like myself, who never saw their name on the honor roll, deceivingly "act" to their students as if they had it all together when they attended school. **Honesty with your students is one of the keys to improving your self-image. Be yourself - the *real* you!**

I don't want to give you the wrong idea about my academic accomplishments, but I always try to word things in the most positive way. So, let me summarize my academic merits this way: *I was in the half of my high school graduating class that made the upper half possible!* Even though I try to put some of my past in a humorous perspective, my negative self-image regarding academic potential was something I experienced personally. I really didn't *think* I could do it, so I didn't do it! **A negative self-image in any area of our lives determines our actions and performance.**

When you start *believing* the negative things others say to you and about you, it paints a poor "picture" - self-image - of yourself. When these thoughts and negative beliefs become fixed in your mind and convince you "this is the real me" - you are treading in dangerous, shark-infested waters. **All our behavior and personality is a result of the picture we have of ourselves.**

For example, if you think you are boring and no one is interested in what you have to say, you will remain relatively quiet in group settings, because you will "act out" the picture you have of yourself." If you did not participate in sports in high school and you "see" yourself as not very athletic, you will be very hesitant to try a new sport, even as an adult, until your picture of yourself changes.

We become the person
we think about most.

The most destructive, fixed beliefs are not only the ones others have helped form - even though they are very dangerous - but the ones you apply to your "self" by *"negative self-talk."*

All feelings and emotions you have are determined by the messages you give yourself! In our internal dialogue, we average 45,000 words per day of self-talk. Sadly, 77% of what most of us say to ourselves is negative and self-defeating. An even more alarming statistic is: It takes the body 24 hours to recover from only five minutes of negative thinking and negative self-talk.

We play thousands of negative self-talk tapes in our mind every day, such as:
"**I can't** . . . do word problems in math . . . make the team . . . get a date . . . get a job . . . speak to large groups of people . . . be a funny person . . . have a positive relationship with my spouse and/or children . . . do bulletin boards . . . be a highly successful teacher."

You will learn how to replace your negative self-talk thoughts with more rational, healthy thoughts . . . *instantly* . . . before you finish this chapter!

Too often, someone makes a statement about us or to us and we accept his or her opinion as fact. Remember: When someone tells you something it is simply his or her opinion of you. Sometimes they are basing it on one specific situation. For example, if you failed an English test and the teacher told you, "Based on the results of this test, you are obviously not going to be a successful teacher," it is only his/her *opinion* of you. **There is a big difference between failing a test - or anything else in life - and *being* a failure.** Did you get that? Did you underline or highlight it?

"Failure is an *event* - *not* a person. Yesterday really did end last night. Today is a brand new day, with new opportunities!"
Zig Ziglar

Beginning today, *refuse to allow someone to put a label on you.* Don't use negative self-talk to put the label on yourself. *Labels are just dressed up excuses* for not breaking out of our comfort zone and really doing something worthwhile in our life. Labels are endless, such as, "I'm too . . . poor, short, tall, fat, skinny, spastic, stupid, ugly, quiet . . . The list is endless." Don't make excuses! Most of them are just labels you have allowed yourself and others to place on you and they are not true. You can do things you thought were impossible when you drop the labels and excuses and see yourself as the valuable person you are. **You deserve to be successful. Believe you can do it!**

During the morning break of facilitating an in-service program, a teacher very emotionally shared his life-story of the impact of labels and the results of really believing them. He told me his senior class yearbook staff gave senior superlatives, such as: most likely to succeed, class clown, best dressed, most athletic, etc. As a joke, he was listed in the yearbook as, "Most Likely to Fail."

Of course he went along with all the laughter, but said inside it hurt him so badly - that his classmates would think, even in a humorous manner, he would never accomplish much in life. The result? It took him over 20 years of failed relationships and numerous jobs before he understood this *powerful principle of not believing the negative labels people place on us.*

Maybe you haven't been *labeled* in a yearbook, but others have helped you paint an unhealthy picture of yourself in one or more areas of your life. You need to daily remind yourself:

Who I "see" is who I'll be!

A teacher, who sees him/herself as not being in control of a class, will truly live every day "out of control" and always be frustrated by continually "putting out fires." **Our actions are consistent with our self-image**. If you want to change your day, change the way you "see" yourself performing during the day. See yourself in control of that hard-to-control student or class.

A teacher who "sees" himself as not connecting with or not having good rapport with his students, will prove this "picture" to be correct by his behavior, such as; rarely joking with students; not volunteering for clubs or activities, that require interaction with students; or perhaps using a classroom management style similar to the military through very little informal talking. His actions back up the picture he has of himself and guess what? He is exactly right. He really doesn't have a very positive connection with students. Who he "sees" is who he'll be.

A study aimed at pinpointing the difference between happy and unhappy people concluded that the single most important difference between the two groups were that "happy people were successfully involved with others while the unhappy people were not."

Low self-esteem, because of a poor self-image, acts as a "roadblock" on the journey of success. It keeps us from involving ourselves with the *right* people: Not just *other* people, but also the *right* people. Many people with a poor self-image are very involved with others, but the *others* are negative, sarcastic gripers who just want them to "join the club." To improve your success potential, regularly associate with people who possess a success mentality and share your goal of wanting to get the most out of life!

Change the mental picture of yourself and you will change your behavior.
Change your behavior and you will experience success!

See yourself as the way you would like to become and begin acting as if you were already that person! It won't be long until you won't have to think about acting that way because it really will be you!!

In their personal life, a teacher may "see" an inadequate spouse or parent, seemingly "never doing anything right." (Ever thought or been told that one?) If so, you will act like the sort of person you "picture" yourself to be. Each time you make even an insignificant mistake, it will further convince you that your "picture" is true. It is the foundation of your entire personality, behavior and even the circumstances you remain in. They are all built on your self-image.

Who do you see yourself to be? Write 2 sentences describing the kind of person you see yourself to be. Not what you *want* to be. What are the strengths and areas of concern in the picture you have of yourself?

Now look at your areas of concern and decide if they are real or beliefs you formed because of what others have said, or perhaps your own negative self-talk that has convinced you they are true. You must truly believe you can change every concern and challenge you have listed into a positive strength.

> ***"What your mind can conceive***
> ***and your heart can believe,***
> ***YOU CAN ACHIEVE!"***
>
> **William James**

The great news is YOU CAN CHANGE! The key is to change your beliefs about yourself. You must believe you can change your self-image by thinking and believing differently about yourself. Belief means daily working at improving these areas.

If it is to be . . . it is up to me!

When your self-image improves, your entire life improves! When it happens, it is so exciting! Think about it. If you want a better life, then change your self-image. It's not easy but is simple and it *can* be done. Yes, YOU can do it!

The results? Teachers who were first considering "early retirement" and later improved their self-image, not only changed their retirement plans, but found such a new lease-on-life, and for the first time in many years, are excited and actually look *forward* to Monday morning! (You read that correctly - "look *forward* to Monday morning!") How long has it been since your "enthusiasm-juices started flowing" on Sunday night because you were anticipating Monday morning at school?

It will take some imagination. In fact, imagining things is one of the best ways to begin forming new pictures of yourself in your mind. Do you remember your early elementary school years when your teacher would ask, "What would you like to be when you grow up?" Without closing your eyes, you were able to instantly "see" - imagine yourself successfully doing almost anything. What happened to that "picture" of yourself you formed in your mind when she/he asked that question?

Animals have a *survival instinct*. This is why squirrels, that were born in the spring, and have never experienced winter begin storing nuts and acorns in the fall, so they will have food during the winter.

Humans have a *<u>success instinct</u>*. You know you want to be as successful as possible and *this instinct is driven with imagination.* Stop - right now. Imagine some specific situations "when you grow up" (or retire.) What would you like to do? Where would you like to travel? Those future plans must begin TODAY! Make the changes necessary to make it become a reality! Begin by writing them down, then imagining them in detail-every day. (Your personal "how-to" plan for reaching your life's dreams and goals will be described in chapter 3.)

Humans always act and perform to whatever they imagine or "see" to be true. <u>Your nervous system cannot tell the difference between an *imagined* experience and a *real* experience</u>. Whatever you "think or imagine" to be true, your nervous system will react to. Again, it doesn't know the difference between what "picture" of yourself you have imagined or thought to be true, or what is actually happens. Both are just as real. Feed your mind thoughts that paint a positive picture of yourself as being successful and you will automatically react as if your are!

People who are hypnotized are told to "imagine" their hand is hot. Tests have proven their skin temperature actually goes up and in many cases a blister will actually form. All because they "imagine" they feel hot.

Professional athletes use "picture visualization/imagination" to prepare for every game. Exceptional basketball players pause before they shoot each free throw and "see" (imagine) the ball going through the hoop before they ever shoot it. They had imagined it happening so many times before the game, their mind and nervous system follows through with the information already there. It doesn't know the difference between reality and what is imagined.

Teachers can use this "success imagination" in the same way. Think of one of your students who present a real challenge to you almost every day. (I realize you possibly have several, but let's focus on one at a time.) Imagine specific behavior habits he/she has demonstrated and mentally *see* yourself acting in a specific way that gives you control over the situation. Be very specific in your imagination: what you will say, your facial expression etc. This is not a one-time exercise. Do this every day, improving each time. Eventually your picture of controlling the situation will become a reality, but not until you "see" it becoming a reality.

Think about the success you want to "see" in your life. Imagine it several times each day as if it were really true. When your actions and habits change it will become a reality.

In order to "see" yourself as a more successful person, you must first imagine it already happening. You must *expect* it to happen. *Expecting* yourself to become a winner at school and at home is an important factor in actually *becoming* a winner. Have high expectations of yourself and don't let negative people bring you down. Sometimes this requires drastic action. **Do whatever is necessary to make a positive change**.

One teacher shared with me that everyone at the faculty lunch table griped from the moment they sat down until they finished eating. She was in a bad mood for her afternoon classes and didn't get nearly the work done in class she planned for. She took action. She decided it was important to keep in touch with her peers, but decided she could do it individually at another time, so she started bringing her lunch and eating in her classroom.

Don't start screaming and yelling - yet. I am not suggesting you do this. Social fellowship with your colleagues is very important to working as a team. I *am* suggesting thinking about what kind of input is being put in your mind during the day - positive or negative - and who/where it comes from. Realize **you will act on the picture that has been painted of yourself and others**.

Typical scenario: You are eating lunch with other teachers and one of them says to you, "If Susie Q. is in your class this afternoon, you better watch out, she is in rare form and is going to give you a fit." Odds are, Susie Q. could do the least little thing and you will act or overreact. Why? Because you have painted a picture of what she will be like today and will look for actions to back up your "picture" of her. **Accept others the way they really are.** In doing so, you will also improve your own self-image.

A healthy self-image is based on positive *self-worth*. You are worth more than you can imagine because you were created in God's image and, as one first grader told her teacher: **"God don't make no junk."** In fact, it is an insult to our Creator to say we are unimportant and unworthy or incapable of accomplishing great things in life. He doesn't create failures and He is responsible for creating you!

Important Self-Image Principles

Instructions: Write these principles on index cards. Choose a different card each day. Carry it with you and quickly glance at it every opportunity you have. (As busy as you are, you will be surprised how many times you will be able to read your "thought-for-the-day.") You will still have "one of those days," but it is amazing how the number of "great days" will increase by doing this. What do you have to lose? Nothing. Try it. It works!

- I have unique talents and abilities and will accept and appreciate the ways I am different from others.
- I will not compare myself to others. There is no "standard" of a perfect person or teacher to judge myself by.
- I understand what others say to me or about me is only their *opinion* and *not reality*.
- I know I have the personal power to make choices that can change my personal and professional life by changing the "picture/self-image" of myself.
- I will "let go" all blame and resentment for wrongs done to me and forgive people. I will stop making excuses and take control of my choices in the classroom and at home.
- I will forgive myself for past mistakes and stop mentally "beating myself up."

- I understand no one "owes" me anything, because it is a debt that I will never collect. I will not let others control my happiness and success.

- I will not take everything personally and will look for the good in my students, peers, family and friends; instead of the wrongs or how I have been slighted.

- I will begin a personal wellness program. My health is important to me.

- I will "dress-up" at least one time a week - when I don't usually do so - because I know the better I look, the better I will feel about myself.

- I will look for something humorous that happens in my classroom and will share it with someone every day. Laughter is the first sign of a positive self-image especially the ability to laugh at myself *when* I make mistakes. Did you watch the movie *What About Bob*? It's not about education per se, but *is* about making progress and being successful. Bob's psychiatrist told him he must **"take baby-steps."** Don't expect your world to change overnight. Be willing to do the little things that make a big difference. Do more than read and underline or highlight important success principles in this book. *Experience* them using a proven plan of action.

At the end of each chapter, you will be given a specific plan of action to begin practicing immediately. These are the "baby-steps" that will lead to your "10-Day Personal Power Plan of Action" at the end of the book. In order for the "10-Day Personal Power Plan of Action" to be effective and make a positive difference in your life, complete the Plan of Action at the end of each chapter.

Strategy #1 Plan of Action

1. What is Teacher Success Strategy #1? (The title of Chapter One.)

   ____

   ____

2. List 6 successes you have already experienced. 3 of these should be personal, (such as - been married x number of years, am a good cook or won a pen for perfect attendance at church), and 3 should be professional, (such as - graduated from college majoring in education, named head of a school committee (leadership), or selected or recognized by my school or class to . . .)

   ____

   ____

   ____

   ____

   ____

   ____

3. List 4 important qualities you offer people in your life. Ex. patience, empathy, etc.

   ____
   ____
   ____
   ____

4. List 4 people, or groups of people, you sincerely care about:

   ____
   ____
   ____
   ____

5. Write 2 things that happened in the past 2-3 days, at home or school that struck you as being humorous.

   ____
   ____

6. Read "**My Personal Commitment Promise**" out loud, every day before you leave home and before you go to bed in the evening. Place a check mark below when you have done so each day: (Copy this on one or more of your index cards. Leave one in a convenient place in your bedroom or kitchen and one on your classroom desk or work area.) Reminder: The more often you read these qualities, the quicker they will become a reality for you. Read all of them every day and you will begin making them become truth.

1st Week

Monday	__a.m.	__p.m.
Tuesday	__a.m.	__p.m.
Wednesday	__a.m.	__p.m.
Thursday	__a.m.	__p.m.
Friday	__a.m.	__p.m.
Saturday	__a.m.	__p.m.
Sunday	__a.m.	__p.m.

My Personal Commitment Promise

I, ______________________________________, am an honest, intelligent, optimistic person who is enthusiastic about my possibilities in life! I am a hard working teacher who is energetic and a team player with members of my faculty, students, and family. I am teachable and want to learn every day how to be the winner I was meant to be! My family and friends are important to me and I will make special time for them every day. I am motivated to do my best so that my healthy self-image will remain on solid ground. These are the qualities, which enable me to be the right kind of person, to do the right things, to have more success tomorrow than today! I AM COMMITTED TO MAKING IT HAPPEN!!

The significance of improving our self-image and thinking the right thoughts for success relate to each other very closely, but are two separate strategies for a reason. We must know our self-worth and value, (Chapter One), before we change our thinking and establish a positive mind-set for success, (Chapter Two). All the positive thinking in the world won't improve your life if you don't first, *Unleash Your Personal Power with a Dynamic Self-Image!*

Now that you have taken that first big step on your journey of success, *are your excited about leaning how changing your thinking can change your life*? *ARE YOU* REALLY EXCITED?!!
If so, say, "***YES, I AM EXCITED!!***" You have to think it to make it happen! While you continue to mentally paint a positive picture of yourself every day, get ready for the second Strategy for Highly Successful Teachers . . .

Change Your Thoughts and You Can Change Your Life!

"S U C C E S S"

"To laugh often and love much; to win the respect of intelligent persons and the affection of children; to earn the approbation of honest critics and endure the betrayal of false friends; to appreciate beauty; to find the best in others; to give of one's self; to leave the world a bit better, whether by a healthy child, a garden patch or a redeemed social condition; to have played and laughed with enthusiasm and sung with exultation; to know even one life has breathed easier because you have lived. This is to have succeeded!"

Ralph Waldo Emerson

"I am aware of people's feelings and I sense you're experiencing a great deal of stress in your life... would you like to talk about it?"

by Chris King

"I don't mind that my son is making more money then I did my first year of teaching. What bothers me is he is only six years old and it's his allowance!"

Teacher Success Strategy # 2

Change Your Thoughts and You Can Change Your Life!

As I sat down with my fellow teaching colleagues at the opening general session of the conference for educators, the keynote speaker was just getting wound-up:

"If you will just *think* positive thoughts, you can do *anything* you want to do!" he enthusiastically exclaimed – as he jumped two feet up from the stage. He continued, "There isn't anything you cannot do if you put your mind to it and think positively. Anything is possible if you just think positive thoughts."

Being the "Doubting Thomas" teacher I was at that time in my teaching career, I began to play the devil's advocate in my mind. "Let's see – he said if I just think positive thoughts, I can do anything. Okay, if that's true, when I return home I can go with my two teenage sons, Jon and Chris, to the school gym, and if I think positive thoughts I will be able to slam-dunk the basketball, just like the NBA players. All I have to do is think positively."

I'm sure you get my point. In fact, there is a high probability you have attended in-service meetings or conferences for teachers yourself and been very doubtful of motivational speakers who promote the possibilities of positive thinking. (Weren't you sitting beside me on the back row, reading the *USA Today*?)

Since then, my understanding of exactly what the speaker was trying to say has changed. He was correct in emphasizing the importance and necessity of thinking the right thoughts and having the right beliefs in order to be successful.

However, he was only telling part of the story. In addition to having a healthy self-image, (as you discovered in Teacher Success Strategy #1), and thinking the right way, (this chapter) - success also depends on important factors such as: managing stress, classroom management skills, working toward personal and professional goals, how to motivate yourself and your students and follow a specific daily success plan – **all of which you will learn in this teacher handbook for highly successful teachers!**

Understanding our self-image, as we discovered in the first chapter, is of vital importance before we discover how exciting it is and how to change our thinking. Applying the exciting, life-changing success principles in this chapter without understanding your self-image, would be like a baseball player hitting the ball and instead of running to first base, decides to cut across the pitcher's mound and head for second base. You must touch first base, Success

Strategy #1, before going to second base, Success Strategy #2. (Take a minute to review the key points you highlighted in chapter one.)

"My heart is singing for joy this morning! A miracle has happened! The light of understanding has shone upon my little pupil's mind, and behold, all things have changed!"
Annie Sullivan, American teacher of the deaf

"I was only a little mass of possibilities. *It was my teacher* (Annie Sullivan) who unfolded and developed them . . . She never since let pass an opportunity . . . to make my life sweet and useful." Helen Keller, American writer

2 Important Factors of Changing for Success

1. Realize the power of your thoughts and beliefs determine who you are and who you can become!

2. Believe you CAN change your life by changing the attitudes of your mind!

"The biggest discovery in our generation is that human beings, by changing the inner attitudes of their minds, can change the outer aspects of their lives!"
William James, Psychologist
Harvard University

Everything you are up to this point in your life, and everything you will become, is the sum total of your thoughts. (Don't miss this powerful success principle – read it again.)
Do you want to improve the quality of your personal and professional life? Then, improve the quality of your thoughts. (You'll discover *how* in this chapter!)

You are probably familiar with Special Olympics, the outstanding organization involved with helping people experience success. One of their brochures states . . . **"It's ALL About Attitude!!!"**

Think about how powerful that statement is! When you consider any area of your life – physical, mental, spiritual, financial etc. – **how successful you will be, is completely determined by your attitude.**

After I share the following thoughts of Chuck Swindol with teachers, titled "Attitude," I have more requests for a copy of it than anything I share during my training sessions. (If *that* many people requested my books, I would be writing this one from the Caribbean Islands - instead of Virginia!)

ATTITUDE

The longer I live, the more I realize the impact of attitude on life. Attitude, to me is more important than facts. It is more important than the past, than education, than money, than circumstances, than failures, than successes, than what other people think or say or do. It is more important than appearance, giftedness or skill. It will make or break a company . . . a church . . . a home.

The remarkable thing is ***we have a choice every day*** ***regarding the attitude we will embrace for that day.*** *We cannot change our past . . . we cannot change the fact that people will act in a certain way. We cannot change the inevitable. The only thing we can do is play on the one string we have, and that is our attitude.*

I am convinced that ***life is 10% what happens to me and 90% how I react to it.*** *And so it is with you.* ***We are in charge of our attitudes!!***

Reread the phrases in bold type. Your attitude really is *your* choice. Just like choosing between a banana split and a hot-fudge sundae with extra nuts, **you will choose your future by choosing your attitudes.**

"Now wait just a minute, Jerry," you may be thinking. "You're telling me that my bad situation at home is because I *chose* it? Why, if I would have known my spouse was going to become the good-for-nothing loser in life he/she is, I would have never gotten married."

"And how about the terrible class my principal gave me this year? I thought last year's class was bad, but this is *definitely* the worst group of kids I have ever had in my umpteen years of teaching! My principal assigned me the most rude, lazy, disrespectful students in our school. Believe me, if I had a *choice*, I wouldn't be teaching this class!"

"What about my health problems? You think I have a *choice* about this nagging lower-back-pain I feel every time I walk around the class?"

Whew! Take a big breath, come back to earth, and really listen to what the word *choice* means – in relationship to your success in life. What it ***does not mean*** is – you have a choice as to the tough hands of cards you are dealt in school and life – such as your health, family situations or students. (Although we *do* have more choices than we realize and sometime want to admit.)

What it ***does mean*** is your answer to the question, "What are you *doing* with the tough hand you have been dealt?" Are you sitting around in the teacher's lounge or cafeteria griping, or are you looking for something good in the people and situations at school and at home? Do you have an attitude of apathy and poor old me, or one of . . .

I refuse to lose!

Let me ask you three questions about choice. 1. Do you think there is something you can specifically do in the next ten days that would make your personal and professional life *worse*? 2. Do you think there is something you can specifically do in the next ten days that would make your personal and professional life *better*? 3. Do you believe every choice you make has an end result?

If you answered "yes" to each question, you just said, **"Regardless of what has happened in the past or is happening now in my life, I believe there is something I can specifically do *right now* that can change my future. The choice is mine!"**

Please rewrite the following statement:
"My future at home and at school depends on the choices I make about situations and people. I will make the changes necessary to become the winner in life I was created to be!"

____

____

One of the sure signs of a person with a right attitude is a healthy sense of humor. In case you are looking for another reason to have a positive attitude, read what a teacher told me following an in-service session:

A positive attitude may not solve all your problems . . .
but it will *annoy* enough people to make it worth the effort!

We may not know the formal definition of a person with a *negative attitude*, but we know one when we see and hear one. They are the people who look like they were weaned on a dill pickle or like the Cruise Director on the Titanic. Of the many "characteristics" they possess, two of the most obvious are *complaining and blaming.*

<u>*The Chronic Complainer*</u> complains about *everything!* You know the people at home or on your faculty and staff I am speaking about, don't you? Whatever happens, they will find something bad about the situation and/or person.

For example, if you were walking with this person to your cars in the school parking lot and they found a $20 bill, instead of being excited about being $20 richer, they would pick it up, turn to you and say, "I can't believe it's *only* a twenty. Seems like it could be at least a fifty!"

A teacher told me about a lady on her faculty whose husband was given a FREE trip for two to Hawaii. When she returned to school, all she did was complain about the trip – the airport, food, hotel, weather, etc . . . and the trip was *free*! Know anyone like that? I don't know how you feel, but I would love to take a free trip to see how the rain looks in Hawaii!

I traveled to a football game last fall with a group of people and quickly observed that one guy, Lenny, seemed to be the President of the National Gripers Club of America. Almost every sentence he spoke was negative. We stopped at a rest area and as some of us were commenting on how beautiful the fall flowers were, I casually joked, "I'll bet $10.00 that Lenny could even find something negative to say about these gorgeous flowers."

One gentleman replied, "As negative as Lenny is, I don't think even *he* could think of something bad to say about these flowers." He pulled out a ten-dollar bill, laid it on the hood of the van and said, "You're on."

As Lenny was walking toward us I shouted, "Can you believe how beautiful these flowers are?" Without even breaking stride, he replied, "Yeah, they're pretty now, but in another two weeks they'll all be dead!" I picked up my friend's ten-dollar bill, smiled and said, "Thank you, Lenny. I hope you're having half as wonderful day as I am." (By the way, I'm not a "betting man," but do consider myself a good business person. I won't pass on an opportunity to receive a 100% return on an investment in less than five minutes.)

One bad apple can spoil the whole basket. One of the problems with hanging around complainers is, if you aren't careful, they will quickly suck you in – just like a vacuum. Ever notice how one teacher can make a negative comment to several teachers about something and within seconds the entire group has jumped on the "complaining bandwagon?" It's like dominos – you push one and they all fall down.

Caution: On a scale of 1-10, where do *you* rate on the frequency of the "complaint scale?" Complaining is easy to do. In fact, it can be downright fun sometimes, especially if we laugh while doing it. It seems so harmless.

However, complaining on a regular basis can be very dangerous to your attitude and thought patterns for success. Ever known someone who is very negative, complains constantly and is still very respected by teachers and students and considered a highly successful teacher? They don't exist.

Why? Teachers can't possibly be positive and enthusiastic about making a difference in students' lives while at the same time constantly complaining and griping. The two simply don't go together. And some things *must* go together. Peanut butter and jelly *go together.* Macaroni and cheese definitely *go together.* But *complaining and becoming a highly successful teacher do not go together.*

☑ **Please place a checkmark beside the items you have complained about during the past week:**

✓ Weather	___ Teachers' Responsibilities
✓ Family/Friends	✓ School Meetings
✓ Responsibilities at home	___ Student's Parents
___ Teachers' Salaries/Benefits	___ School Administrators

Professional counselors and psychologists report it is not only okay, but also healthy to express and "open-up" our emotions in an appropriate way at an appropriate time - to someone we have confidence in. But there is a difference in venting our emotions, disappointments and feelings, and constantly complaining.

For example, throwing your eraser and chalk at a disrespectful student during class would *not* be an appropriate way to express your anger. (I have found pouring water and the entire contents of a 20 gallon aquarium over their heads works much more effectively. Just kidding. Please do *not* highlight that statement as a strategy for highly successful teachers – even if you *would* feel better afterwards.)

Success Strategy for Decreasing Complaints:
Choose two blank index cards from your pack you are using to write positive quotes and thoughts on. At the top of one of the

index cards write the words **Complaint Card.** At the top of the other index card, write the words **Compliment Card.** Begin to be aware of your complaints and compliments and keep a record by writing a tally-mark on the appropriate card when you say either one. You will be amazed how, after only one or two days, you will begin to "think before you speak" regarding the impact, (positive or negative), of what you are going to say.

Helpful Hint: I suggest *not* telling your class you are doing this. Some students would possibly get a real kick out of intentionally trying to "send you over the edge," (worse than they usually do), just to make you add three or four marks to your Complaint Card. As in, "I'm getting sick and tired of this class acting like a bunch of . . ." (You know how the rest of it goes, right?)

Keep a record of your complaints and compliments for 5 days and you will find yourself; in a better mood, more upbeat and energetic, getting more things done, and more fun for others to be around – at school and at home. *It works – do it!*

I've observed teachers experiencing results that were so dramatic they could hardly believe it themselves. One teacher said he actually went through an entire day without making one single complaint, and said it was the best day of teaching he had in over ten years!

Another teacher who apparently was a member of a faculty with numerous negative attitudes, challenged – and to her surprise they accepted – her faculty to start a "Gotcha Jar." Everyone was a good sport and agreed when someone caught another faculty member complaining about something or someone they would say,

"Gotcha" and the guilty party would put fifty cents in the Gotcha Jar. At the end of the month, they used the "proceeds" and met one morning before school at a local restaurant and enjoyed a delicious buffet breakfast – and a lot of fun.

You may be thinking, "With all the complaining I hear from the teachers on our faculty, after only one week of using the Gotcha Jar, we would probably have enough money to send everyone on a one week cruise to the Bahamas!" (Hey - maybe this is a good idea after all.)

Even if *everyone* doesn't join the fun, you can do this with just a few people. If you wait until *everyone* on your faculty participates in "fun" activities, you may wait a long time. Be a leader and let the others see what they are missing by not participating.

> **"Don't let the things you *can't* do, interfere with the things you *can* do!"**
>
> John Wooden

In addition to the *Chronic Complainer*, another easily identifiable negative person is the *Badmouth Blamer*. Blaming other people began many years before your school was built or you were born. In fact, the first record of blaming someone else is found in the Bible.

God told Adam and Eve, "Enjoy life, but don't eat anything from the tree in the middle of the garden." Of course, just like your students, they did exactly what they were *not* supposed to do. Sound familiar?

One evening God was hiking through the garden and asked Adam why he ate the fruit. Adam replied, "Well, there's this woman, Eve, *she* made me eat the fruit." As Zig Ziglar says when explaining this story, "We all know the real problem wasn't the apple in the tree, but the "pair" on the ground."

Blame and justify. Blame and justify. When we blame others, as Adam did, for our circumstances, we are not accepting responsibility. **Successful people begin by accepting responsibility for their situation then start an action plan and do something about it!** They refuse to blame people for their situation.

It's not where you *start* that matters,
it's where you *finish*!

Some teachers **"If"** themselves to death. We all have our favorites. What are some of yours?

"**If** I had a better home situation . . ."
"**If** I had a better principal . . ."
"**If** I had better students . . ."
"**If** I had more supportive parents . . ."
"**If** I made more money . . ."
"**If** . . . **If** . . . **If** . . ."

Blaming our lack of success in any area of our life on these or other factors is a cop-out to facing the situation and making a decision to do something about it.

Before my mother passed away, after a courageous five-year fight with cancer, she gave a soul-searching talk to many church groups titled, "*Bloom Where You Are Planted.*" She shared how everyone faces challenges in life, but how we overcome these challenges, *instead of blaming others*, (especially people who had nothing to do with our situation), is the sign of a person who will accomplish great things in life.

Blaming or complaining has never made people or situations improve. In fact, they have more of a negative affect on our daily performance than you can imagine. Both dramatically affect our *thinking* – and *that* is exactly what Teacher Success Strategy #2 is about.

Discover for yourself why *how we think* is so important. The September 15, 2000 issue of *Investor's Business Daily* featured the following list of the traits of successful people - including teachers – possess. *T*raits that **can turn your dreams into reality**. (Trait number one is described in this chapter and traits number two and three are described in the next chapter.)

Secrets to Success

1. **How you *think* is EVERYTHING!** Always be positive. Think success, not failure. Be aware of a negative environment.

2. **Decide upon your true dreams and goals.** *Write down* your specific goals and develop a plan to reach them.

3. **Take action.** Goals are nothing without action. Get started now. Just do it.

Numerous teachers have responded and found how it was a "simple but major breakthrough" to understand the following simple explanation of how our mind works and how it affects our success in life. *Get your highlighter ready because* **you are about to discover the super-charged principles of how the thoughts in your mind decide your degree of success in life!**

In chapter one I asked, *"Are you interested in getting more out of your personal and professional life?"* Are you? I mean do you REALLY want to live life to it's fullest? If you really do . . . **putting the principles in this chapter into action can literally *change your life* – both in the classroom and at home!**

Change Your Thinking and You Can Change Your Life!!

How do we think? Your brain is very similar to a computer. If you put incorrect information in it, the output processed on your printer will also be incorrect. Even for a non-computer person like myself, I remember this was originally referred to as *Garbage In, Garbage Out.*

Just like a computer, when negative information is processed by your brain, there is a high probability your thoughts and behavior will be negative – negative talking, (such as complaining and blaming), negative facial expressions, and negative attitudes towards other people and life's situations.

Negative input (information) never results in positive output (behavior).

People who seem negative to you – consistently blame and complain about school and life – have made a *choice* to focus more on the negative than the positive aspects of situations. Their negative behavior is a result of choosing to look for the negatives. Many people don't understand they really do have a *choice* as to what they do with the hand they are dealt. What are you doing with your situations such as personal problems or poor performing students? Are you looking for the positive? Are you looking for the good in your family and students?

I love the story about little Billy, who was so positive that no matter how bad a situation seemed at the moment, he always thought something good would eventually happen, to the extent that his father actually got tired of his overly-optimistic attitude and thought Billy had crossed the line of just being downright unrealistic. "Everything in life is not good," he would say to his son. To prove his point, one of the Christmas presents he gave Billy was a box of pony poop.

As soon as Billy opened the box and saw the contents, his eyes opened wide, he smiled and immediately ran outside and began looking in the garage and in the yard . . . everywhere. His father followed him and asked, "What in the world are you looking for?" Billy, forever the optimist, excitedly exclaimed, "Well, if one of my presents is a box of pony poop, I just *know* there's got to be a little pony somewhere around here for me!" (Wouldn't it be a better world if we all had Billy's attitude and thinking?)

Just like a computer, you can *change* your output (behavior) by *changing* your input (information). In other words, you can experience more success in life when you *choose* to consistently - every day - put positive things in your mind instead of negative. The key success principle for you is the word *choice*.

You choose and change your thoughts and behavior by choosing and changing the information you feed your mind. Consistently change the information you are listening to, reading and watching and your behavior will change! Is that exciting or what?!!

Listed below are seven sources of information used to feed your mind. Please place a check under one of the columns indicating whether you think the information from that source is *More Negative or More Positive*:

	Source	
	More Positive	**More Negative**
1. Television	____	____
2. Newspaper	____	____
3. Books	____	____
4. Radio	____	____
5. Other People's Conversation	____	____
6. Your own Self-Talk	____	____
7. Computer	____	____
8. Other: ________________	____	____

If you watched the 6:30 evening news lately, out of approximately 24 stories, how many do you think focus on the positive aspects of life? If you guessed 1-3, you are correct. During a typical day at school, do you think your mind hears more compliments and motivational information from other teachers, students and administrators, or more complaining, blaming and criticizing? Remember – garbage in, garbage out.

Highly successful teachers hear and see just as much negative information as other teachers. The key difference is . . . highly successful teachers **choose**, (there's that word again – *choose*), to focus on the good stuff and put positive information in their minds to replace the negative.

How much negative stuff is in there? Research tells us that by the time you and I graduated from high school, we heard 175,000 negative comments. "Don't do this . . . You can't do that . . ." We also know **it takes twelve positive statements to replace one negative statement.** We have a challenge every day to focus on the positive, but it's an exciting challenge. This is the very difference between highly successful teachers and teachers who finish their careers in apathetic, ho-hum mediocrity.

Information

↓

Thoughts/Beliefs

↓

Behavior/Performance

Choose to change the information you put in your mind and your thoughts, beliefs and behavior will change!
(Change your input and you will change your output.)

Have you ever done something so many times, you did it without even thinking about it? For example, do you arrive at school some mornings and don't even remember actually driving part of the trip? You don't remember actually making a specific turn or passing a certain store because you were actually thinking about something else? Your body was doing one thing – driving – while your mind was concentrating on another subject?

This is a phenomenal function of our success-thinking process accomplished by using our **subconscious mind**. We use our **conscious mind** when we are aware of what we are doing. But by doing something repetitiously, our subconscious mind is programmed to do it without consciously thinking, "I am doing this."

I remember my dad teaching me how to drive our car, a 1962 Opel, (so long ago they don't even make them anymore), which had a straight-shift, manual transmission. As a teenager, driving a vehicle that required "changing the gears" was cool, but really difficult to learn. The first several times I drove, I really concentrated on how to let the clutch out while at the same time, pressing just the right amount on the gas pedal. If I didn't "kill the engine" or scrape the gears, the ride was so jumpy the car moved like it had a bad case of the hiccups.

But after several months experience with driving the car, I rarely thought about the proper procedure of working the clutch and gas pedal. I would just start the car and take off without even thinking about it. (My wife says I *still* drive like this.) If you had a similar experience, understand that when you reached the point where you didn't have to think about the mechanics of driving, your *subconscious mind* took over and you just *did* it. What does this have to do with being an effective teacher?

Your subconscious mind is a key to you becoming and remaining a highly successful teacher! Why? Because by following the action plan you are about to learn, you can reprogram your mind to eliminate the negative stuff that is possibly there now.

Remember: You can *choose* to change your thoughts to a right-way of thinking for more personal and professional success, but you must first *want to change,* and second *take action - by doing the things necessary for change!*

2 Simple Steps for Changing to Success Thinking: Stop and Start!

STOP! Stop complaining and griping about people or situations beyond your control. Change the things that you can control and learn to adjust to the things you can't control. Since your actions are a result of the kind of thoughts you think, you will act negatively when you speak or think negatively. Words you say are first thought of in your mind. **Stop -** Before you say something to/about someone negatively, and think, "Is this going to help or hinder the situation? Will this comment build them up or tear them down?" Barney Fife, the one-bullet deputy on the old Andy Griffith Show, sums it up by saying, "Nip it in the bud."

**If what you are going to say is negative –
don't say it!**

Stop – as much negative information as possible from entering your mind. On a typical day at school and home, what sources are you depending on for most of your information? (Refer to the list on page 60). For example, you may not be able to leave a predominately negative faculty meeting, (now *there's* positive thought, right?), but you *can* monitor what you hear on the radio, see on television, and read in the newspaper.
To live a more positive life, change your thoughts by changing the information that is entering your mind!

Stop – listening to or watching the news, or reading it in the newspaper to start or end your day! Research shows **the first major encounter your mind has for the day will have more impact on what kind of day you have than the next five encounters combined**! Make your first daily "thinking encounter" a positive one! How?

<u>START</u>: Start listening to a positive tape or read something positive for the first 10 minutes and the last 10 minutes of your day! Don't *have* the time? It's a matter of priorities. No one has an "extra 20 minutes" every day. But, if I know doing this consistently will help me change my life for the better, believe me, I will *find* the time and a way to do it. I discovered how to do this without trying to fit it into my already hectic, busy schedule.

Success Suggestion: Daily listen to a tape of someone you personally feel gets you "fired-up" for the day, or gives you some positive thoughts to sleep on. (For your use, I have included a list of tapes and books of some of the most dynamic and helpful success trainers known today, in the back of the book.) If you don't have a portable cassette player with headphones, you can purchase one for around $15.00, (even cheaper at a yard sale or flea market), and set it in a place that is easily accessible to you when you get up in the morning or getting ready for bed.

Personally, I use it while I am shaving each morning. Female teachers tell me they use it while they are putting on their makeup. I realized if I am going to "just stand there" a few minutes every day, that's valuable time I could use to put positive information in my mind, without taking up any "extra" time.

The same principle applies to listening to a success tape while you are driving to and from school. How valuable are the words to the songs or the conversations of some of the talk shows in helping you deal with the tough stuff you must mentally be prepared to face for the day? Use at least part of your driving time to mentally prepare yourself for the day and to unwind at the end of the day in a positive manner before you return home. **You will find you sleep better** – even if you have had "one of those days." It really works! Remember: *Positive In - Positive Out*.

How many consecutive meals have you missed in your life? What would happen to you if you didn't eat physical food for several days? Loss of energy, headaches, and the loss of your ability to function properly are among the many ways you would be affected. The same is true with the necessity of a daily positive *mental* diet! You cannot wait until you are stressed, frustrated and depressed to begin your positive diet. **Your mind must be fed success thoughts <u>every</u> <u>day</u>**, so you will be able to overcome the challenges at school and at home you will face – **<u>every</u> <u>day</u>**!

Listening to positive success thoughts "once in awhile" won't lead you to success. Some people say, "That positive thinking, motivational stuff only works for a short time." They are exactly right, but guess what? A daily diet of positive thinking and a motivational thought program of action will allow you to do so much more in life than if you don't do it!

Motivation is like taking a bath...
You can't do it just one time and expect it to last forever!

Success Suggestion No. 2: Use *positive self-talk affirmation cards*. What you hear others say will affect your thoughts and behavior. But *what you say to yourself* is of equal importance in programming you mind for success! **To improve your quality of life, you *must* replace your *negative self-talk tapes* with positive ones.**

In chapter one, *Teacher Success Strategy #1* began our success journey by emphasizing the necessity of playing positive tapes of your self-image – thinking about things you *can* do. After beginning the mental construction project of improving your self-image – the mental picture you have of who you really are – apply the principles of *Teaching Success Strategy #2 and begin a* daily action program of replacing the negative tapes you have played in your mind for many years with *positive* tapes.

The most effective, life-changing way to do this is use *positive self-talk affirmation cards*. It is one of the most dynamic and effective ways I know to change your thinking. And the best part . . . no one has to even know you are doing it! It's not like going on a diet when your friends and family notice you aren't eating and ask, "What's wrong with you?" You can begin putting this success principle into action, without any pressure from anyone – TODAY!

As I suggested in chapter one, *please use your index cards*. Begin looking for positive quotes and statements on tapes you listen to, read in this book or other resources. Write each statement on an index card and use one card per day to program your subconscious mind. Read it several times during the day and make a goal of trying to memorize it before going to bed.

Technology is a wonderful learning tool. But repetition is still the mother of learning. I learned my multiplication tables by participating in my teacher's use of "flash cards." Over and over and over . . . This is how we put information in our subconscious mind for "automatic recall for future use." The same success principle applies to feeding your mind positive success thoughts. **When you are in a stressful, negative situation, you can't *recall* information unless it has been previously placed in your subconscious mind**. Positive Affirmation Cards (PAC) are a great way to do this!

I have several stacks of cards in rubber bands. I take one card off the top of the stack and carry it with me to review several times during the day. The next morning I return it to the bottom of the stack and take the next card for my "positive affirmation for the day."

Don't leave home - or your desk - without it! One teacher shared how he was surrounded by faculty members who were constantly negative. He carried his PAC, (Positive Affirmation Card), with him all day, to use as *ammunition* against negative comments and thoughts. When people would start griping and complaining, he would quietly and quickly, without anyone noticing, glance at his PAC for a morale boost for the negative situation.

Positive Affirmation Cards (PAC) are your way of repetitiously putting positive information in your subconscious mind, so you eventually reach the point you don't have to think about *trying* to be positive – *you will be positive!* (Remember the earlier example of the more times you drove a car with a manual transmission, the less you thought about it and *just did it?*) Just like driving, the more you "practice" being successful, (by mentally feeding your subconscious mind on positive information), the more often you will *act* positively – at home and school - without even thinking about it! Thousands of successful people have experienced it. **It works for them and it will work for you!**

Positive Affirmation Cards will have more affect on your thinking and self-talking than anything you plan to do. (You still need to do the other parts of the success plan.) Remember: **When your thoughts and beliefs change, your behavior will change, and the most effective way of changing your thoughts and beliefs is through the repetition of positive information!**

Follow this action plan for fifteen days and you will begin to see a different person when you look in the mirror! Your gray hair – or no hair – condition may still exist, but it won't matter as much because **you will begin to change and improve where it matters most . . . from inside your mind and heart!**

Key Success Principles of Strategy #1

1. Improving your quality of life is truly *ALL about attitude*!

2. You have a *choice* of what you will do with your situation in life!

3. *Stop* complaining and blaming!

4. *Start* reprogramming your subconscious (success) mind by using Positive Affirmation Cards, listening to positive tapes, and reading motivational literature.

Success Strategy #2 Plan of Action

1. Write Success Strategy #1:

   ____

   ____

2. Write Success Strategy #2:

   ____

3. List 2 specific things you will *stop complaining* about – beginning today.

   1. ________________________________
   2. ________________________________

4. What success training tape will you listen to first? (Your favorite, or refer to the resource list on page 186):

   ____

5. If you do not have a supply of index cards, (to use for Positive Affirmation Cards), when and where will you purchase them? ______________________________

6. Name two people you have found it difficult to communicate with, in a positive manner - one in your personal life and one you teach with. Make a commitment to smile and ask them how they are doing. (Listen to their answer.) Write their initials or a code word, if you prefer not to write their name in your handbook.

   ____

WOW! You are making great progress on your new journey of success! You are forming a more positive mental picture of yourself – self-image – and are working on a personal plan of action to change your thinking from failure to success!

While continuing to be a winner in the areas of self-image and positive thinking, you are now preparing to take the third step of improving your personal and professional life by learning how to manage stress and teacher burnout. Success Strategy #3 – **Strangle Stress and Extinguish the Fires of Teacher Burnout** – will help you learn how to be successful, even when you have "one of those days . . . or weeks . . . or months . . . or . . ."

At this point, you know I expect you to make a positive affirmation that you are ready for the next dynamic strategy to become a highly successful teacher. Managing stress is the next important step on your journey of personal and professional success. Are you ready? Please answer enthusiastically, **"YES – I am ready!!"**

GREAT! LET'S GO!

> "Teaching kids *how* to count is fine, but teaching them *what* counts is best."
> Bob Talbert

Teacher Success Strategy #3

Strangle Stress and Extinguish the Fires of Teacher Burnout!

"I've *had* it!" you say to yourself. "I've *had it* up to *here* with all the papers I have to grade! I have *had it* with all the meetings! I have *had it* with all the extra "duties!" I have *had it* with discipline problems, state mandated tests, low pay, unsupportive administrators and parents, and I have ***definitely*** *had it* with rude, obnoxious, apathetic students, who don't really care whether they do well in school or not! I used to actually enjoy teaching, but it's just not worth it anymore. First chance I get . . . I'm 'outta here!"

Sound familiar? It wouldn't be quite as serious if teachers contemplated these thoughts at the *end* of 'one of those days' and only 'once in awhile.' But many teachers find themselves in this mind-set before they leave home or on the way to school – on a regular basis.

To make matters worse, you finally arrive at school and . . .

You're late for bus duty because you couldn't find your car keys or matching shoes;
Taking the "shortcut" to school at 85 mph, you noticed the gas tank was below empty;
Somehow, you made the "landing" in the parking lot on fumes, and as you run to the cafeteria, two students are fighting on the floor as your principal stands in the door looking at her watch, as if to say, "You do know this is going in your permanent performance file, right?"
After taking roll at the beginning of your first class, the assistant principal walks in and informs you he will be observing you during the next hour and asks to review your lesson plans for the day. For five minutes you frantically and unsuccessfully search for them when suddenly it hits you . . .they are at home on the kitchen table!
About 10 minutes into the observation, one student boldly asks, "Why are we doing all this written work so early? You usually give us "free time" and we don't ever do anything for at least 20-30 minutes?" (You look for a hole in the floor to drop through. There is none.)
Following the student's comment, your assistant principal immediately begins writing intensely and fills at least 3 pages in his yellow legal pad – which you know *is not a good sign.*
Except for a student throwing up at the table beside you during lunch and a fire drill in the pouring rain, you somehow make it to the end of the day.
The bell rings and just as the last student leaves your classroom, the principal says those magic words on the PA system, "All teachers are reminded of the extended faculty meeting this

afternoon in the library. We have some very important things to discuss so be prepared for the meeting to last until at least 6:00 p.m."
Somehow you endure 2 ½ hours of discussing such "important" things as whether to serve Coke or Pepsi at the next parent open-house and who would like to serve on the committee for the special community program to be held year after next.
As you finally pull in the driveway, your entire family is waiting on the front porch and you realize this is Family Night Out for Pizza.
You drag yourself and your forty-five pound book-bag out of the car as one of them yells, "Why are you late? You only work until 3:30. It seems like you could at least respect our plans enough to get home on time!"
You fall on your knees in the yard and sob uncontrollably as you hear someone ask, "What did I say? All I asked was why were you late?"
They leave for pizza without you. It's the only good thing that's happened all day!!

Hopefully, you don't have too many days like the one just described. But odds are if you have taught for at least one week, you have experienced days when you were so stressed out you wondered whether it really was worth all the hassles of being a teacher.

One of my passions and mission of this book is to help you experience a life of happiness and fulfillment with less worries, doubt and stress. A life that will help you reach more of your potential, as a person and a teacher.

I have great news for you. **You were meant to enjoy life . . . NOW – not just after retirement!** That's right. You were meant to enjoy your career as a teacher, but you must understand the effects of stress on your life. Unmanaged stress can dramatically affect you at school and at home.

How serious are the effects of stress on your personal and professional life? The following facts confirm that it can literally be a matter of life and death. That's about as serious as you can get!

There is a growing body of medical research that implicates stress with our health. As Sgt. Joe Friday used to say on the television show *Dragnet*, "Just the facts":

- Stress is the number one factor in heart disease!
- 95% of all tension headaches are caused by stress!
- 90% of all teachers say they experience stress at least 2-4 times per week!
- Stress has passed the common cold as the most prevalent health problem in the U. S.!
- Stress contributes to 8 of the top 10 causes of death among Americans!
- 65% of patient visits to family practice physicians or internists have nothing to do with medical diseases. The symptoms are real, but the cause of the symptoms is *stress*!

Needless to say, the personal toll of stress on you personally and as a teacher is dramatic! In addition to it's affect on your health, some of the consequences of not properly managing stress include: absenteeism, inadequate time spent preparing lessons, less patience assisting students who need additional one-on-one help, and strained family/personal relationships.

Before we see where we are going, we must first know where we are. Completing the *Teacher Stress Self-Assessment* is a great starting point to focus on your specific areas of concern.

Please complete the following *Teacher Stress Self-Assessment.* Write the letter of your choice to indicate how often, during the past year, these issues created stress for you.
Key: N = Never, S = Sometimes, O = Often

Teacher Stress Self-Assessment

Personal Stress:

___ 1. Your own health or the health of family or friends
___ 2. Marriage or relationships with others
___ 3. Moving out of a place of residence
___ 4. Your household/family responsibilities
___ 5. Vacation
___ 6. Lack of time spent with family or friends
___ 7. Lack of leisure-time for yourself
___ 8. Death of someone close to you

Job-Related Stress:

___ 9. My job as a teacher is demanding and creates tension
___ 10. I feel tired and not physically ready for work
___ 11. My schedule or teacher responsibilities create problems
___ 12. I experience conflict with students, other educators and parents
___ 13. I changed teaching jobs or major responsibilities (one time = "S")
___ 14. I miss work because I need a mental break or have personal problems

___ 15. Generally speaking, I feel my job is boring and unchallenging

___ 16. Generally speaking, I feel the morale at our school should be better

___ 17. Generally speaking, I don't see very much humor/laughter in my life

Total Number of "S's": ____ Total Number of "O's": _____

There isn't a "magic number" that would indicate whether you are experiencing too much stress. But if your total number of "S's and O's," (when added together), exceeds 8, you could be in the *danger zone* and need to take the action steps given in this chapter to manage stress and take better control of your life.

"Teacher Stress is . . ."

- Losing your grade book 2 days before report cards are due
- Remembering you left the class pet at school over spring break
- Teaching a computer class to students who know more about computers than you do
- Setting your alarm clock on "p.m." instead of "a.m." the first day of school
- Your worst student returning to your classroom as a student-teacher
- Having the superintendent's or school board chairperson's child in your class
- When a student wants to know if his parent's lawsuit against the school district will affect his grade
- Having to borrow lunch money from your students

- Grading a complete set of tests – using the wrong answer key
- When the school nurse shows up at your classroom to perform a head lice check
- Leading the committee for textbook selection
- After counting students on a school field trip, coming up one short
- Finding out your students' best achievement test scores are the lowest in the school
- Hearing one of your "discipline-challenging students" say, "My dad wants a conference with you tomorrow morning and he is *really* mad!"

(*Erasing My Insanity*, Kimberly Chambers)

What do you *really* know about stress – other than you are fairly certain you experience it frequently? All stress is not bad. *Eustress* is the kind of euphoric sensation experienced when your favorite team is trying to win in the final seconds of the game. Just like the athletes, your adrenalin is flowing and you are excited. You are nervous and experiencing stress, but it affects you positively. In fact, just like the athletes, it is possible to perform better when you experience eustress. You probably experienced eustress your first day of teaching or on your first day of college classes.

Distress is the kind of unpleasant and/or harmful sensation experienced when faced with *too much to do and not enough time to do it.* For example, *distress* occurs at the end of a grading period when you are trying to complete your report cards. The pressure is on and you are not a happy camper. Since teachers seem to experience more *distress* than *eustress* at school, Teacher

Success Strategy #3, **Strangle Stress and Extinguish the Fires of Teacher Burnout,** will help you manage your negative distress levels at home and school. Remember, stress at home *does* affect your performance in the classroom.

When I drive my car and the gas gauge on the dashboard starts flashing "Low Fuel," it is a warning signal to me that if I don't refill the tank soon, I will be thumbing a ride to the nearest service station. (Actually, it's not a *service* station. Remember when gas stations used to really *service* your car?) Just as the gasoline gauge signals a warning regarding the fuel level in my car, our body gives us warning signals to slow down and take care of it. If we don't heed the warning signals, we will pay the consequences listed earlier.

Some of the warning signals our body gives us include: increased tension headaches, loss of energy and enthusiasm, impatience, quick temper, rapid pulse, insomnia, fatigue, and loss of appetite. Have any of these warning lights been flashing in your life lately? Refer to the *Teacher Stress Self-Assessment* you completed earlier and circle the number beside each statement you marked as "O" = Often. Focus on those specific areas during Teacher Success Strategy #3.

My family lives in the southern part of Virginia in a small rural town near the beautiful Blue Ridge Mountains. During the winter we usually have enough snow accumulation to close schools several days. When this happens, because of the obvious danger involved with hazardous road conditions, my brother-in-law, who is a dedicated policeman in a nearby town, doesn't exactly look forward to driving during the night shift patrol. (I don't blame him.)

On the other hand, my wife Lucy, a dedicated elementary teacher for 27 years, has an entirely different reaction. As much as she loves students and enjoys her work, she absolutely goes bananas when she hears those magic words, "All schools will be closed today." (Can you relate to her elation and joy?)

What is the difference between the reaction of my brother-in-law and my wife? Same situation – snow – but two completely different reactions. My brother-in-law's stress level increased, but Lucy's stress level decreased. The difference? Their <u>*perspective*</u> or how they viewed the situation.

> "We might cease thinking of school as a place, and learn to believe that it is basically relationships between children and adults, and between children and children."
>
> George Dennison

Our *perspective* of situations – not the situation itself – is the deciding factor in our stress level. It is our perspective – how we "see" things - that results in either endless, energy-draining *worry* or just *concern* about a situation. Psychologists report that 80% of the items on our "worry list" shouldn't be there, for two reasons:

1. We can't do anything about the situation.
2. The situation we're worrying about isn't going to happen.

Personally, I have wasted a lot of good brain cells worrying about something, ("What if . . ." only to realize later the potentially bad situation I was worrying about didn't even happen. Sometimes referred to as, "Making a mountain out of a mole hill.")

Imagine for a moment you are the parent of a teenager who is completing their first semester of college. (Maybe you are like me and don't have to *imagine* – those tuition bills are for real!) You've been thinking things are going okay this semester until one day during the first week of December, you receive the following letter in the mail:

Dear Mom and Dad:

Please sit down before you read this letter. (You already know this isn't going to be good news, right?) *I'm doing okay now, since the dormitory fire, thanks to the loving care of our custodian, Norman. You see, Norman more than pulled me from the fire – he has become my entire life!*

Yes, we're living together now and I know you will learn to love him as deeply as I do. Oh yes, one more thing – my pregnancy is now beginning to show. I know how thrilled you must be, considering how much you always wanted to be a grandparent.

Your loving daughter,

Mary

P. S. There was no fire. I'm not pregnant and, in fact, there is no Norman. However, this semester I am going to flunk Biology and just wanted you to put it in it's proper perspective!

As you read the letter, didn't you begin to think the situation was continually getting worse? What if you really *did* receive a similar letter from someone? Would you "keep your cool" or have a "heebie-jeebie fit" in the middle of the floor?

Dr. Richard Carlson, in his series of books, *Don't Sweat the Small Stuff: It's All Small Stuff,* tells us to ***"Stop living in the emergency zone!"*** In other words, every thing that happens in your life that is not planned, is not a national emergency. Learn to *go with the flow.*

During my first year of teaching I met a teacher on our faculty who was so structured he would mentally "lose it" when we had a fire drill. He allowed something as small as one 10-15 minute time segment to completely blow him out of the water the rest of the day. As the students said to him, "Mr. Franklin, get a life!"

Like Mr. Franklin, many people fail to recognize the causes or *Triggers of Stress.*

Stress Triggers

At School:

- ***Recent Events*** such as major *changes* in policies or procedures; requirements to work more hours per week than normal; sudden significant increases in the activity level or pace of work; major reorganization.

- ***Ongoing Conditions*** at school such as too much work to do in too little time; feedback only when performance is unsatisfactory; temperature in your classroom; noise; interruptions; meetings after school hours; deadlines;

conflicts between you and students or coworkers; unclear standards and expectations, etc.

Away from School:

- ***Recent Events*** such as restriction of social life, marriage, death of someone close, serious illness, etc.

- ***Ongoing Conditions*** such as personal finances/bills; anxiety and worry about your children's activities; your career plans, etc.

Each of the *Stress Triggers* can throw us into a mental state of anxiety and *frustration.* So, what can you do to handle frustrations?

F ind the unresolved issue. *All frustrations are the result of an issue you haven't completed.*

R evisit the issue and figure out why it wasn't resolved. Face the issue.

U nderstand the fears you attached to the event.

S tay focused on finding the resolution.

T ake it at a manageable pace. Slow down and walk, not run.

R efuse to walk away until you have solved the problem.

A sk for help if you can't get it done on your own. This shows you are serious.

T ruth is critical. Most people aren't honest about their emotions and frustrations.

I nternal discipline is a must. Many people talk themselves out of finishing.

O pen yourself to being challenged.

N ever procrastinate. I repeat . . . **Never procrastinate!** Whatever problems are causing your frustrations, don't put off your game plan for solving them. Do it – TODAY!

(Source: Richard Flint Seminars)

List 2 situations that are causing frustration in your life and one step you will take immediately to start solving each problem:

1. Situation

____

____

Action Step:__________________________________

2. Situation:

____

____

Action Step:__________________________________

Worry . . . Worry . . . Worry . . . Worry . . .

Use the *5-5-5 rule* for deciding which frustrations to worry about. Ask yourself this question: "<u>In 5 weeks, 5 months or 5 years, will worrying about this situation really make any difference in my life?</u>"

As you consider your situations, remember that worry and stress are caused by our *perspective*. What if you received the following letter from your child, who is attending summer camp?

Dear Dad and Mom:

Our scoutmaster told us to write to our parents in case you saw the flood on TV and worried. We are OK. Only 1 of our tents and 2 sleeping bags got washed away. Luckily, none of us got drowned because we were all up on the mountain looking for Chad when it happened. Oh yes, please call Chad's mother and tell her he is OK. He can't write because of the cast. I got to ride in one of the search and rescue jeeps. It was neat. We never would have found him in the dark if it hadn't been for the lightening.

Scoutmaster Webb got mad at Chad for going on a hike alone without telling anyone. Chad said he did tell him, but it was during the fire so he probably didn't hear him. Did you know that if you put gas on a fire, the gas-can will blow up? The wet wood still didn't burn, but one of our tents did. Also, some of our clothes burned, too. John is going to look weird until his hair grows back.

We will be home on Saturday if Scoutmaster Webb gets the car fixed. It wasn't his fault about the wreck. The brakes worked okay when we left. Scoutmaster Webb said with a car that old you have to expect something to break down; that's probably why he can't get insurance on it. We think it's a neat car. He doesn't care if we get it dirty, and if it's hot, sometimes lets us ride on the tailgate. It gets pretty hot with 10 people in a car. He let us take turns riding on the tailgate until the highway patrolman stopped and talked to us.

Scoutmaster Webb is a neat guy. Don't worry. He is a good driver. In fact, he is teaching Terry how to drive. But he only lets him drive on the mountain roads where there isn't any traffic. All we ever see up there are big logging trucks.

This morning all of the guys were diving off the rocks and swimming out in the lake. Scoutmaster Webb wouldn't let me because I can't swim and Chad was afraid he would sink because of his cast, so he let us take the canoe across the lake. It was great. You can still see some of the trees under the water from the flood. Scoutmaster Webb isn't crabby like some of the scoutmasters. He didn't even get mad about us not wearing our life jackets.

He has to spend a lot of time working on the car so we are trying not to cause him any trouble. Guess what? We have all passed our first aid merit badges. When Dave dove in the lake and cut his arm, we got to see how a tourniquet works. Also, Wade and Jamie threw up yesterday. Scoutmaster Webb said it probably was just food poisoning from the leftover chicken. He said they got sick that way with the food they ate when he was in prison. I'm so glad he got out and became our scoutmaster. He said he sure figured out how to get things done better while he was doing his time.

I have to go now. We are going into town to mail our letters and buy some fireworks. Don't worry about anything. We are doing just fine.

Love, Cole

Yes, there are things we should legitimately be concerned about and need to take action. But many things should be placed on the "back burner" – or completely off the stove. For many situations in our lives, *especially those we have no control over*, we need to remember the words to the song . . .

Don't Worry, Be Happy

"You say your rent is late, the landlord is going to li-ti-gate,
Don't Worry, Be Happy.
There's no place to lay your head, they're gonna come and take your bed,
Don't Worry, Be Happy."

There **is** a positive side of being stressed . . .

"Stressed, spelled backwards is . . . Desserts!"

There is one person who will make the important decision about what perspective to take on situations and how "stressful" it will be. It's the same person who is responsible for your self-image. And it's the only person on earth who is responsible for the level of success you reach in life . . . YOU! So, understanding how to manage stress is a part of understanding yourself. Have you ever done something and later thought, "Why did I act that way?"

One of the most powerful ways of understanding yourself and how **you can "manage yourself" for <u>more success and less stress</u>** is using the *DISC Profile*. This dynamic self-assessment has been used by schools, Fortune 500 companies and leading organizations for over 20 years in over 35 countries! The reason it is used worldwide is simple: **It works!** Personally, understanding the DISC Profile has been a great benefit in helping me deal with the frustrations and stress of life and in successfully relating to people different from me.

Different Strokes for Different Folks

As you read *and highlight* the descriptions of DISC, remember that understanding who you are will help tremendously in managing stress and your relationships to students, colleagues, family and friends. The purpose is not to put you in a slot or box, (as in, "you are a D or an I" etc.), but to help you realize **you are naturally made up of certain characteristics that all blend together to make you the unique and valuable person you are!**

Many teachers will have one or two areas they are dominant in, but everyone is a unique combination of all 4 parts of DISC. (You are not *either* a D or I or S or C, but a blend of each.) I can't wait for you to see yourself in DISC. **Look - and you will find <u>YOU</u>!**

<u>DISC Profile of Behavior Tendencies</u>

Do you consider yourself generally to be:

- *Fast-Paced* – outgoing, takes risks, takes action, enjoys talking/telling, *or*

- *Slow-Paced* – reflective, reserved, avoids risks, thinks through decisions

Do you consider yourself generally to be:

People-Oriented – share opinions and feelings, relationships are important, *or*

Task-Oriented – plan their work, consider facts/data for decisions

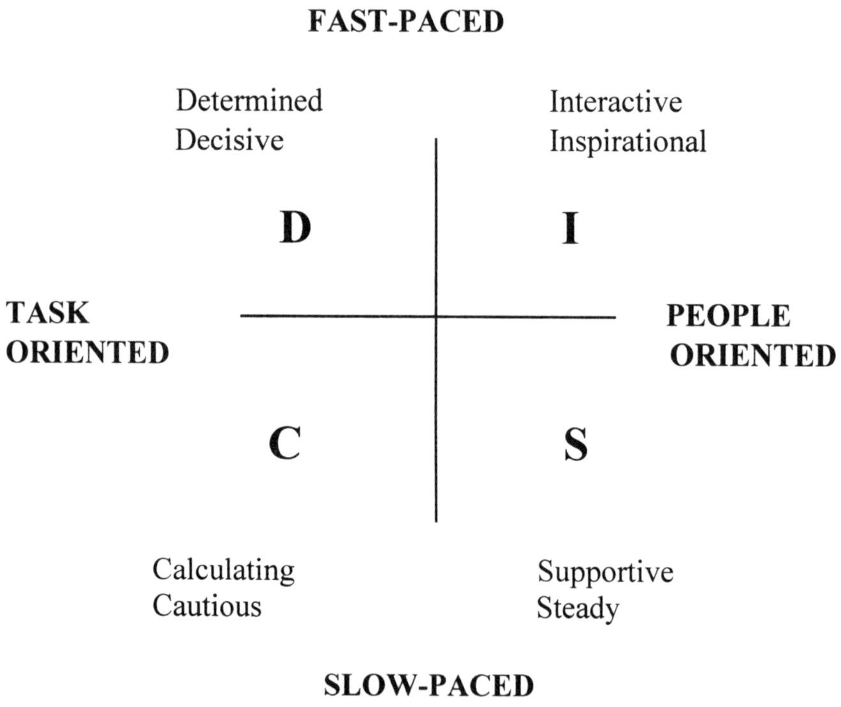

FAST-PACED

Determined
Decisive

Interactive
Inspirational

D **I**

TASK ORIENTED **PEOPLE ORIENTED**

C **S**

Calculating
Cautious

Supportive
Steady

SLOW-PACED

You have determined if you are basically: fast-paced or slow-paced and whether you are people oriented or task oriented. ***After reading the description of behavior tendencies of DISC below, write a number beside each of them, according to which describes you the most. (#1 = the tendency that describes you most; #4 = the tendency that describes you least.)*** For example, after reading all the descriptions, if you feel the "I" describe you best, write a 1 beside the "I." If the C describes you second best, write a 2 beside the C, and so on.

You will most likely see words in all four descriptions that may apply to you, but after further consideration you will be able to discover one or two that are more like you than the others. Again, no one tendency is *better* than the other and **there is no one category that most teachers *should* be**. Some of the most highly successful teachers have high tendencies in "S" or "C", (slow-paced) and are not described as outgoing or talkative. Don't think, "Since I am a teacher, I *should* be a . . ." Be honest about who you really are. When you do, *your stress levels will decrease dramatically*! **(Don't forget to rank as 1, 2, 3, or 4.)**

___ **D** = Dominant, Driving, Demanding, Determined, Decisive Doer
(Fast-Paced and Task-Oriented) Likes to take charge of situations, sometimes it's *"My way or the highway,"* as in *"These are **my** class rules and we aren't voting on them."* Has very few discipline problems in class.

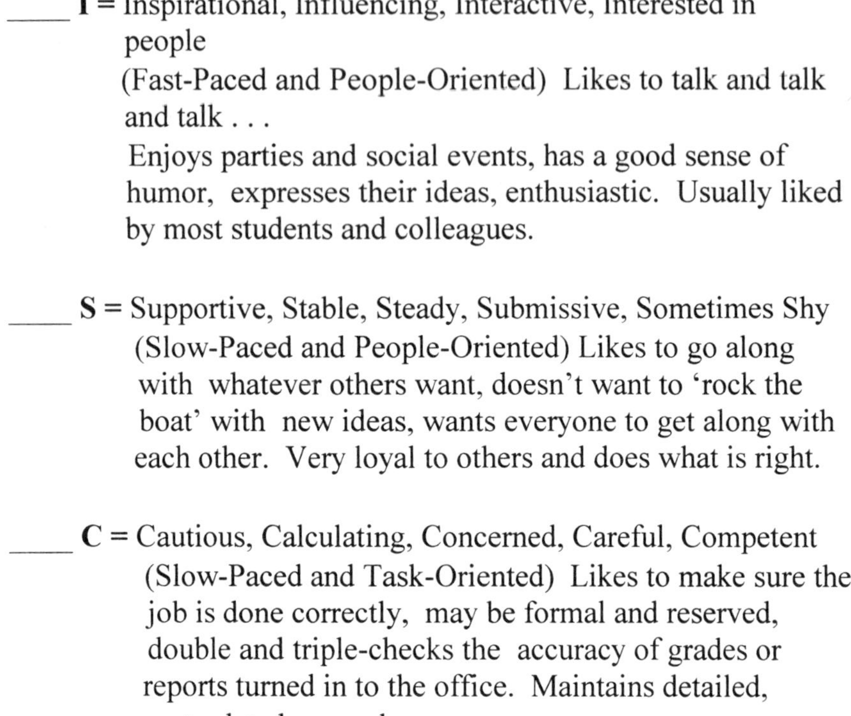

____ **I** = Inspirational, Influencing, Interactive, Interested in people
(Fast-Paced and People-Oriented) Likes to talk and talk and talk . . .
Enjoys parties and social events, has a good sense of humor, expresses their ideas, enthusiastic. Usually liked by most students and colleagues.

____ **S** = Supportive, Stable, Steady, Submissive, Sometimes Shy
(Slow-Paced and People-Oriented) Likes to go along with whatever others want, doesn't want to 'rock the boat' with new ideas, wants everyone to get along with each other. Very loyal to others and does what is right.

____ **C** = Cautious, Calculating, Concerned, Careful, Competent
(Slow-Paced and Task-Oriented) Likes to make sure the job is done correctly, may be formal and reserved, double and triple-checks the accuracy of grades or reports turned in to the office. Maintains detailed, up-to-date lesson plans.

Do you "see yourself" in the DISC Profile? If you feel 2 of the areas both describe you equally, then give them both the same ranking number. Another advantage of understanding yourself with DISC is you should stop comparing yourself to others. Trying to "measure-up" to them causes a ton of stress. **Be YOU!**

Faculties at schools have a lot of fun with the DISC profile. Once everyone understands the main characteristic of each one, you begin to not only realize ***your*** high tendencies, but also begin to associate them with your colleagues' tendencies.

For example, think of someone on your faculty who comes to school a month before the school year begins - puts up all their bulletin boards – prepares lesson plans for the entire first semester – and runs copies of all their tests and quizzes for the first grading period. (Maybe a *little* exaggeration, but you get the point.) If you were to look up the words *organized* or *doing-it-by-the-book* in the dictionary, you would find their picture. Learn about yourself and others using DISC, but **have some fun** with it and don't take yourself too seriously.

Speaking of fun – yes, learning **should** be enjoyable – let's look at the humorous side of DISC. **One of the most effective ways of reducing stress in your life is the ability to laugh at yourself! LAUGH!**

DISC Humor

Grocery Shopping and DISC:

D is an impulse shopper and never has a list.

I tells you where everything is in the store, whether you ask or not.

S is prepared with a list and goes up and down each aisle in a consistent and orderly fashion, the same way he or she has for the last 10 years.

C has coupons and a calculator and can tell the cashier if there has been a mistake ringing up the sale.

<u>Parent-Teacher Conferences and DISC</u>:

D hands the parent the student's final grade and ends the conference.

I discuss all of the student's interaction with others, but isn't quite sure what grade the student is getting.

S has a copy of every worksheet and paper the student has turned in this grading period and wants to discuss each of them with the parent.

C has a printout of every score the student has received the entire school year and a detailed list of each item that was wrong on every quiz and test and keeps an up-to-date grade average on every student every day.

Remember, **each of us has some of all four areas in us, but many teachers *do* have one or two areas they tend to lean toward most of the time.** Personally, I have very high tendencies as an "I" - (I like to talk and talk and talk . . .), and very low tendencies of an "S" or "C.") If you are a high tendency of "S" or "C," (slow-paced person), I am the faculty member to whom you might say, "Jerry, you are always on the go, go, go. Your energy is really getting on my nerves. Would you *please* be quiet, slow down, quit going 90 miles per hour, and for crying out loud stop drinking coffee every morning. You *definitely* do not need any caffeine."

Other *people* can cause *you* stress! Learn to understand how DISC helps you appreciate differences in others. Did you ever think, "I wonder why s/he acts like that?" As a result of learning about DISC, you should understand everyone is made differently, so appreciate and respect his or her differences.

However, this doesn't mean we continue acting in inappropriate ways and convince ourselves it's acceptable because, "I have a high tendency of (D, I, S or C) and just can't help the way I act, so live with it." It teaches us our areas of strength and areas needing improvement for success. DISC can also improve your personal relationships. Think about your spouse, children or friends. In which DISC areas do they have high tendencies? Acknowledging these tendencies can enhance your communication and relationships, and reduce stress at home. The result? You will also experience a more stress-free life at school.

Let's focus on your final game plan of action to help you reduce stress in your life.

Key Principles of Managing Stress and Teacher Burnout

- Stress is caused by our *perspective* of situations, not the situation itself
- We become frustrated and worry about problems because we procrastinate solving them and in our minds make them "bigger than they really are."

- DISC Profile is used to reduce stress and burnout by showing us that our differences are important and help us accept the uniqueness of others

Teacher Success Strategies to Strangle Stress and Teacher Burnout

1. Take action necessary to solve problems at home. They won't "just go away."

2. Be flexible. Go with the flow. Unexpected things *will* happen. Learn to adjust.

3. Don't take everything personally. Everyone is not going to like everything you do or say. It doesn't mean you are a failure. It's just *their* opinion of you.

4. "Don't worry, Be Happy." **Use the 5-5-5 guideline for worrying**.

5. Be prepared. The scout motto relates to *thorough lesson preparation*. Even if you aren't able to accomplish all you wish, the more prepared you are, the better you will be able to handle the unexpected. Set daily goals for outside the classroom – a "to-do list" – and *do it*!

6. Begin a personal wellness program to improve your physical health. The basics of getting plenty of rest, eating

right and exercising are an important part of reducing stress and becoming the winner you were created to be!

7. De-junk your life. Get organized. You can do it. Clean the clutter off your desk, file things that need to be filed, and catch up on grading your papers. **Working *harder* does not reduce stress. Working *smarter* reduces stress.**

8. Accept your mistakes *when* you make them. Not *if* you make them – *when* you make them. Forgive yourself, use it as a learning experience, (I have a *lot* of "learning experiences"), and move on to things that need to be done every day!

9. Continue your personal plan of improving your self-image and feeding your mind a daily diet of "positive thoughts" by listening to tapes or reading . . . every day!

10. **SMILE!** That's right. Don't have anything to smile about? Look for something humorous and you will find it. (Include reading the comics in your daily motivational quiet time.) Look for something humorous every day at home and at school and you will find it! **Humor and laughter are nature's built-in "stress-busters!"**

Teacher Success Strategy #3 Plan of Action

1. Write (from memory) Teacher Success Strategy #1:

   ____

2. Write (from memory) Teacher Success Strategy #2:

   ____

3. Write (from memory) Teacher Success Strategy #3:

   ____

4. What motivational tape or book are you learning from today? _______________________________________

5. List 2 *unimportant* things you have been worrying about, that you will stop worrying about – beginning today.
   A. ____________________ B. ____________________

6. Which behavior tendency in the DISC Profile described you best, (D, I, S, C)?___________________________
   Why? ____

7. What is one specific change you will make to begin living a less stressful life - beginning today?

   ____

As a result of feeding your mind a daily diet of positive thoughts and accepting yourself as you are, (Teacher Success Strategies #1 and #2), you are also beginning to experience a less stressful and more productive life, (Success Strategy #3)!! Don't stop. Practice every day!

The road to success is always under construction!

Please write the following statement: "The first three teacher success strategies are life-changing, and the next three are going to be even better!"

____

____

By completing and continuing to practice the first three strategies, YOU have reached a major milestone in becoming the highly successful teacher and the winner in life you were meant to be! CONGRATULATIONS!

The first three strategies complete Stage I. Continue practicing them daily as you begin Stage II, starting with Teacher Success Strategy #4 . . .

Touch Students' Hearts Before Teaching Their Minds!

If your rocket mind is on the launch pad, it's time for lift off! Are you ready? **Are YOU ready! Ya' gotta mean it when you say it . . .**

"YES . . . I am <u>definitely</u> ready to begin Teacher Success Strategy #4!!!"

Why Do I Do It?

I am a teacher and I find myself asking the same question all the time. Most of the time I do not know the answer, or it is just at the tip of my tongue, waiting to be revealed to me.

Many times I get tired of waiting for the answer and walk off in frustration. Other times I fall asleep pondering the question.

When I am struggling with my checkbook, I ask this question: Why do I do it?

When I am up at 4 in the morning so I can finish typing tests and searching for materials (since we don't have books that match our state mandated standardized test, Standards of Learning), I ask myself this question: Why do I do it?

When I have to stay for meeting after meeting, leaving me no time to fix dinner for my family, I ask myself this question: Why do I do it?

When the child in the last row has thrown a pencil and then a desk at me for the fourth time, I ask myself this question: Why do I do it?

When I am at Wal-Mart buying my own children's clothes off the clearance rack so I can afford the needed paper and scissors for school, I ask myself this question: Why do I do it?

When I spend my evenings taking university classes and my summers at professional-development conferences, I ask myself this question: Why do I do it?

When I have to go to school on Saturdays to do paperwork, I ask myself this question: Why do I do it?

When I hear people blame teachers for the problems in the schools today, I ask myself this question: Why do I do it?

Teaching... Take This Job and Love It!

When I hear people say that teachers have it easy, "they do have the summer off," I ask myself this question: Why do I do it?

When I am looking for a second job so that I can afford to go on vacation, I ask myself: Why do I do it?

When I sit waiting after school for a parent who never shows up for the conference, I ask myself this question: Why do I do it?

When I have to go more than six hours without time to go to the bathroom, let alone eat lunch without gulping it down, I ask myself this question: Why do I do it?

When I am standing at the copy machine at Kinko's because the school has no more paper, I ask myself this question: Why do I do it?

I ask this question a lot. I often have no answer for it. Recently, one of my children recognized me as her teacher in a very special way and the answer became loud and clear to me.

Why do I do it? I do it for the children. I do it for those who show appreciation and for those who do not. The same question is always there, and it is a new gift each time it gets answered again.

Why do I do it? I do it for the children.

By Ann K. Alonso, Teacher

TEACH
ME

> "One looks back, with gratitude, to those who touched our human feelings. Warmth is the vital element for the growing plant and for the soul of a child."
>
> Carl Jung

Teacher Success Strategy #4

Touch Their Hearts Before You Teach Their Minds!

"One Friday, in the classroom, things just didn't feel right. We had worked hard on a new concept all week, and I sensed that the students were growing frustrated with themselves – and edgy with one another. I had to stop this crankiness before it got out of hand. So I asked them to list the names of the other students in the room on two sheets of paper, leaving a space between each name. Then I told them to think of the nicest thing they could say about each of their classmates and write it down.

It took the remainder of the class period to finish the assignment, but as the students left the room, each one handed me their paper .

That Saturday, I wrote down the name of each student on a separate sheet of paper, and I listed what everyone else had said about that individual. On Monday I gave each student his or her list. Some of them ran two pages. Before long, the entire class was smiling. "Really?" I heard whispered. "I never knew that meant anything to anyone!" "I didn't know others liked me so much!"

No one ever mentioned those papers in class again. I never knew if they discussed them after class or with their parents, but it didn't matter. The exercise had accomplished its purpose. The students were happy with themselves and one another again.

That group of students moved on. Several years later, after I had returned from a vacation, my parents met me at the airport. As we were driving home, Mother asked me the usual questions about the trip: How the weather was, my experiences in general. There was a slight lull in the conversation. Mother gave Dad a sideways glance and simply said, "Dad?" My father cleared his throat. "The Eklunds called last night," he began.

"Really?" I said. "I haven't heard from them for several years. I wonder how Mark is." Dad responded quietly, "Mark was killed in Vietnam," he said. The funeral is tomorrow, and his parents would like it if you could attend." To this day I can still point to the exact spot on I-494 where Dad told me about Mark.

I had never seen a serviceman in a military coffin before . . . The church was packed with Mark's friends. (His old classmate) Chuck's sister sang "The Battle Hymn of Republic." Why did it have to rain on the day of the funeral? It was difficult enough at the grave side. The pastor said the usual prayers and the bugler played taps. One by one those who loved Mark took a last walk by the coffin and sprinkled it with holy water.

I was the last one to bless the coffin. As I stood there, one of the soldiers who had acted as a pallbearer came up to me. "Were you Mark's math teacher?" he asked. I nodded as I continued to stare at the coffin. "Mark talked about you a lot," he said.

After the funeral most of Mark's former classmates headed to Chuck's farmhouse for lunch. Mark's mother and father were there, obviously waiting for me. "We want to show you something," his father said, taking a wallet out of his pocket. "They found this on Mark when he was killed. We thought you might recognize it."

Opening the billfold, he carefully removed two worn pieces of notebook paper that had obviously been taped, folded and refolded many times. I knew without looking that the papers were the ones on which I had listed all the good things each of Mark's classmates had said about him. "Thank you so much for doing that," Mark's mother said. "As you can see, Mark treasured it."

Mark's classmates started to gather around us. Chuck smiled rather sheepishly and said, "I still have my list. It's in the top drawer of my desk at home." John's wife said, "John asked me to put his in our wedding album." I have mine too," Marilyn said. "It's in my diary." Then Vicki, another classmate, reached into her pocketbook, took out her wallet and showed her worn and frazzled list to the group. "I carry this with me at all times," Vicky said without batting an eyelash. "I think we all saved our lists."

That's when I finally sat down and cried.

by Helen P. Mrosla, Teacher

Why do you think adults would save a piece of paper they received in elementary school? Two reasons: 1) A teacher did more than "teach" the content, she touched their hearts, and 2) People hunger for encouragement and appreciation. *Highly successful teachers understand that students will work harder for them if they feel appreciated.*

> **Students will forget most of *what* you teach them, but will remember *how* you made them *feel* in your class!**

Most of the time we really do put the cart before the horse. We concentrate on the *teaching* instead of the *touching.* Can you remember a time when your teacher cared more about you as a person than as a student? What a difference it makes when we are encouraged!

Encouraging Words

A group of frogs were traveling through the woods and two of them fell into a deep pit. All the other frogs gathered around the pit. When they saw how deep the pit was, they told the unfortunate frogs they would never get out. The two frogs ignored the comments and tried to jump out of the pit. The other frogs kept telling them to stop, that they were as good as dead.

Finally, one of the frogs took heed to what the other frogs were saying and simply gave up. He fell down and died. The other frog continued to jump as hard as he could. Once again, the crowd of frogs yelled at him to stop the pain and suffering and just die. He jumped even harder and finally made it out.

When he got out, the other frogs asked him, "Why did you continue jumping? Didn't you hear us?" The frog explained to them that he was deaf and that *he thought they were __encouraging__ him the entire time!*

The story teaches us two lessons: 1. There is power of life and death in the tongue. An encouraging word to someone who is down can lift them up and help them make it through the day. 2. A destructive word to someone who is down can be what it takes to kill him or her. Be careful of what you say. Speak life to everyone who crosses your path.

The power of encouraging words . . . it is sometimes hard to understand that an encouraging word can go such a long way. Anyone can speak words that tend to rob another of the spirit to continue in difficult times. Special is the teacher who will take the time to encourage another person.

You will become an influential teacher when you become an encourager. In fact, after you begin the construction project of improving your own self-esteem, (Teacher Success Strategy #1), Phase II - chapters four, five and six - deals with how to help your students improve their self worth.

M. M. F. I.
("Make Me Feel Important!")

This is what each student would like to tell you every day as they sit in their desks in your classroom. When you make them feel significant, their self-worth and confidence will grow. The result?

The Institute of Student Motivation conducted a study that clearly showed the impact of self-confidence on academic achievement is greater than that of IQ!

"Show me the money!" Building self-esteem is *more* than just making students "feel good." The Psychology Department of the University of Pennsylvania discovered that students with high self-esteem are more successful in their careers and *get higher paying jobs* than students with low self-esteem.

If you really desire to help students improve their performance in your classroom and prepare them better for life, then "touch their hearts" by helping them paint a positive mental picture of themselves.

When students know we *really* care about them, we will be able to teach them more by accident than we could ever teach them on purpose!

Most students do not truly believe they can accomplish tough goals in life. Just as we do, they tend to focus on their failures and what they have NOT been able to do. Former UCLA basketball coach John Wooden – who won 7 national championships in 10 years – said, *"Don't let what you cannot do interfere with what you can do!"* Encouragement keeps students from quitting.

A mother who wanted to encourage her young son's progress on the piano, took him to a Paderewski concert. After they were seated, the mother spotted a friend in the audience and walked down the aisle to greet her. Seizing the opportunity to explore the wonders of the concert hall, the little boy rose and eventually explored his way through a door marked "NO ADMITTANCE."

When the houselights dimmed and the concert was about to begin, the mother returned to her seat and discovered that the child was missing. Suddenly, the curtains parted and spotlights focused on the impressive Steinway on stage. In horror, the mother saw her little boy sitting at the keyboard, innocently picking out "Twinkle, Twinkle Little Star."

At that moment, the great piano master made his entrance, quickly moved to the piano, and whispered in the boy's ear, "Don't quit. Keep playing." Then leaning over, Paderewski reached down with his left hand and began filling in the bass part.

Soon his right arm reached around to the other side of the child and added a running obligato. Together, the old master and the young novice transformed a potentially frightening situation into a wonderfully creative experience. The audience was absolutely mesmerized.

Whatever our situation in life and regardless of how hopeless we think our students and class situation may be, remember our Creator is whispering deep within our beings, "Don't quit. Keep playing. Don't quit. Keep playing." *You will discover that* ***when you consistently encourage others, YOU will be encouraged!***

I don't really know exactly what it was, but I always felt my eighth grade history teacher, Mrs. Billig, thought I was important as a person, not just a student. Even though I wasn't exactly on the path to becoming a Rhodes Scholar and didn't "burn any midnight oil" studying at night, if I completed homework for *any* of my classes, it would be her class. Why? Because I knew she cared about me. I simply didn't want to disappoint her.

Making students feel *significant* is a vital part of being a highly successful teacher.

When they feel significant you will be astounded by the effort they make to please you. Don't have time to encourage students? Then don't ever expect them to perform anywhere close to their potential and your expectations of them. Remember, 10% of your students will excel in spite of your attitudes toward them – whether it is positive or indifferent. They are intrinsically motivated. But the performance and behavior of the other 90% depends greatly on the job you do as a nurturer and encourager.

When my two sons, Jon and Chris, were younger, they would always pull for sports teams who were winners. In the 90's the Chicago Bulls were 'the' popular team. But as they grew older and matured, they began supporting teams that were the underdogs. This is typical of many sports fans. It's called "jumping on the band wagon." As long as a team is winning that's 'our' team, but when they hit the rocky road, we switch to another team. It's only natural to associate ourselves with winners instead of losers.

Your students want to be winners too, but don't have any *fans* at home pulling for them. We need to be reminded that with all the problems at home – high divorce rates, alcoholism and abuse – situations aren't the same as 40 years ago. No one stands at the door (because most likely they aren't at home) to ask, "How was your day at school?" When a parent *does* return for the evening they are so stressed out from their own day they often verbally criticize or tear down the student and make them feel unimportant. **<u>YOU</u> are the one person in their life that can give them security and make them feel significant!**

Have you ever taken a class where the teacher really "knows his/her stuff" and it was obvious their intention was to impress everyone with their abundance of knowledge? One of the most important principles of being a highly successful teacher is:

Students don't care how much you know until they know how much you care!

In other words, "touch their hearts" first. Instead of inspiring students to get them to think more highly of you, daily try to help them think more highly of themselves.

There is one signal that tells students very clearly you care for them. There is one sign they will watch for. There is one thing they hope to see, beginning the first day they walk in your class, that you will "make" time to **listen** to them.

The real world of teaching doesn't make it easy or convenient to listen to students. In fact, with your unbelievably hectic schedule you probably feel you hardly have time to take care of your required responsibilities, much less taking time to listen to students, right? You are exactly right. I believe this is one of the greatest challenges of highly successful teachers - to somehow find it in your heart to make time to listen.

And to make it even tougher, guess which students need you to listen the most? The rude, disrespectful students are the ones crying out for help and just don't know the appropriate way to get you to listen to them. It's much easier to make time for the Honor Roll Students, who are doing what we ask of them, isn't it?

But I have never seen a book on success, morals or religious guidelines that instructs us to "only treat people with respect, who respect you first." As success trainer Zig Ziglar rewords the "golden rule" so well:

"You can have just about anything in life you want if you will first, help enough other people get what they want!"

If you are saying to yourself, "I just don't have time to listen to them," then you are exactly right. You – or any teacher – don't *have* the time to listen. But the teachers who make a life-time impact "make" the time. It's tough. It's REALLY tough, but you can do it. Being a successful teacher and leader means doing the things other teachers aren't willing to do. **The benefits of seeing**

students excel and mature will blow you away when you know you have had a part in it! These words say it best:

The Paradoxical Commandments of Leadership

People are illogical, unreasonable, and self-centered – love them anyway.
If you do well, people will accuse you of selfish, ulterior motives – do well anyway.
If you're successful, you'll win false friends and true enemies – succeed anyway.
The good you do today will perhaps be forgotten tomorrow – do well anyway.
Honesty and frankness make you vulnerable – be honest and frank anyway.
The biggest person with the biggest ideas can be shot down by the smallest person with the smallest mind – think big anyway.
People favor underdogs but follow only hot dogs – fight for the underdogs anyway.
What you spend years building may be destroyed overnight – build anyway.
People really need help but may attack you if you help them – help them anyway.
Give the world the best you have and you may get kicked in the teeth – give the world the best you have anyway.

You will be surprised how much comes back to you in return for making the time to listen. I remember one of my college professors, who had a reputation as a highly intellectual person, saying to our class during my freshman year in college, "I look forward to learning from you." We couldn't understand what he meant. *He* was going to learn from *us*? He explained that when we reach a point in life where we as teachers think we know it all and can't learn from our students, it's time to leave the teaching field, go in the locker room, pack our duffle bag and go home. Always listen for things to learn from your students.

The following true story is a powerful example of how, when we make sacrifices and listen, adults *can* learn from students – beginning by "touching hearts":

> "The world talks to the mind. A teacher speaks more intimately; a teacher talks to the heart."
>
> Haim Ginott

Sacrifice Play

In Brooklyn, New York, Chush is a school that caters to learning disabled children. Some children remain in Chush for their entire school career, while others can be main-streamed into conventional schools.

At a Chush fund-raising dinner, the father of a Chush child delivered a speech that would never be forgotten by all who attended. After extolling the school and its dedicated staff, he cried out, "Where is the perfection in my son, Terry?"

Everything our Creator does is done with perfection. But my child cannot understand things as other children do. My child cannot remember facts and figures as other children do. Where is our Creator's perfection?"

The audience was shocked by the question, pained by the father's anguish and stilled by the piercing query. "I believe," the father answered, "that when God brings a child like this into the world, the perfection that He seeks is in the way people react to this child" – *how they touch his/her heart.*

He then told the following story about his son Terry:

One afternoon Terry and his father walked past a park where some boys Terry knew were playing baseball. Terry asked, "Do you think they will let me play?" Terry's father knew that his son was not al all athletic and that most boys would not want him on their team. But Terry's father understood that if his son were chosen to play it would give him a comfortable sense of belonging and self-worth.

Terry's father approached one of the boys in the field and asked if Terry could play. The boy looked around for guidance from his teammates. Getting none, he took matters into his own hands and said, "We are losing by six runs and the game is in the eighth inning. I guess he can be on our team and we'll try to put him up to bat in the ninth inning."

Terry's father was ecstatic as Terry smiled broadly. Terry was told to put on a glove and go out to play short center field. In the bottom of the eighth inning, Terry's team scored a few runs but was still behind by three. In the bottom of the ninth inning, Terry's team scored again and now with two outs and the bases loaded with the potential winning run on base, Terry was scheduled to be up. Would the team actually let him bat at this juncture and give away their chance to win the game?

Surprisingly, Terry was given the bat. Everyone knew that it was all but impossible because Terry didn't even know how to hold the bat properly, let alone hit with it. However, as Terry stepped up to the plate, the pitcher moved a few steps to lob the ball in softly so Terry should at least be able to make contact. The first pitch came in and Terry swung clumsily and missed. One of Terry's teammates came up to him and together they held the bat and faced the pitcher, waiting for the next pitch. The pitcher again took a few steps forward to toss the ball softly toward Terry.

As the pitch came in, Terry and his teammate swung the bat and together they hit a slow ground ball to the pitcher. The pitcher picked up the soft grounder and could easily have thrown the ball to the first baseman. Terry would have been out and that would have ended the game. Instead, the pitcher took the ball and threw it on a high arc to right field, far beyond reach of the first baseman.

Everyone started yelling, "Terry, run to first. Run to first!" Never in his life had Terry "run to first." He scampered down the baseline wide-eyed and startled. By the time he reached first base, the right fielder had the ball. He could have thrown the ball to the second baseman to tag out Terry, who was still running.

But the right fielder understood what the pitcher's intentions were, so he threw the ball high and far over the third baseman's head. Everyone yelled, "Run to second. Run to second!"

Terry ran towards second base as the runners ahead of him deliriously circled the bases towards home. As Terry reached second base, the opposing short stop ran to him, turned him in the direction of third base and shouted, "Run to third." As Terry rounded third, the boys from both teams ran behind him screaming, "Terry, run!"

Terry ran home, stepped on home plate and all 18 boys lifted him on their shoulders and made him the hero, as he had just hit a "grand slam" and won the game for his team.

"That day" said the father, with tears now rolling down his face, "those 18 boys reached their level of our Creator's perfection and taught a valuable lesson by "touching Terry's heart."

(Author Unknown)

Words of encouragement give the power of hope! When I was a kid, I remember hearing the statement, *"Sticks and stones may break my bones, but words will never hurt me."* Whoever came up with that "brilliant" principle of living needs to have their head examined! Nothing can be farther from the truth.

I was speaking at a state conference for school administrators and shared with over 1,400 principals and assistant principals that, "As serious as the situation regarding weapons and violence is in our schools today, discouraging words have killed the spirit of more young people than all the guns and knives together."

Following my presentation, a lady introduced herself while showing me a picture of her son, in his Junior Varsity football uniform. She expressed her appreciation for sharing how powerful the words we say to young people are and the impact those words can have.

She continued by telling me how her son's football coach, who her son had a great deal of respect for, very innocently made a comment to him the week before JV basketball tryouts saying, "You know, you are a fine football player, but you're never going to amount to much on the basketball court." She wondered if the coach had any idea the struggle she had during the next week trying to reestablish some confidence in her son and convince him he should try out for the basketball team. Just a few words, but what a powerful impact.

Choose words that help you be a "dream-maker" - not a "dream-breaker!"

Just for the record, I believe the title of "Coach" is one of the most respected, but misunderstood job titles in education. I am proud to have had some great coaches when I participated in sports in school. A coach is a helper and encourager. You are probably aware that in today's world many people make their living "coaching" people to success. As a student, I had a caring "band coach," "drama coach," "vocational coach," and several "academic coaches" (teachers). They all "coached" me at the beginning of my success journey.

Yes, words are important and what you say will have an impact on students. For fun, let's look at . . .

7 Things You Won't Hear Teachers Say

1. "Our principal is soooooooo smart . . . no wonder s/he is in administration!"
2. "I can't believe I actually get paid for doing this!"
3. "Thank goodness for these evaluations. They really keep me focused!"
4. "It's Friday? Already? This week has just flown by!"
5. "All of our in-service training programs are so exciting!"
6. "We'd be able to better educate our children if they would let us teach through July and only have one week of vacation!"
7. My spouse thinks I'm around the house too much and that I'm not spending enough time at school!"

Below are typical comments of what highly successful teachers **are** saying about the necessity of understanding that course content is a small part of really **"touching hearts and teaching minds":**

"College didn't prepare me for the student whose mother was murdered by a jealous boyfriend; for the student who witnessed a drive-by shooting; for the student who was removed from her/his home because of an abusive father; or for the student who hasn't eaten since lunch in the school cafeteria the day before. These realities do not exist in the textbooks, yet they are too often the realities that many students bring in my classroom. Students are real people with real problems. *How can you expect them to care about your course content until they know you care about them as a person, with all their hurts in life?"*

Have you ever thought about how wonderful it is that everyone doesn't look the same? Think about it. We should appreciate that our individual differences at home, school and in our community are what make us strong as a group. Everyone – even your most difficult students – have something to contribute or bring to the table.

> "We need to fill a child's bucket of self-esteem so high that the rest of the world can't poke enough holes in it to drain it dry."
>
> Alvin Price

The same principle applies to communicating with your students. We must think about their needs and differences and that each of them *has something to bring to the table.*

Remember the Children

Remember the children . . .
Who sneak Popsicle's before supper,
Who erase holes in math notebooks,
Who can never find their shoes,
Who hug us in a hurry and forget their lunch money,
Who spend all their allowance before Tuesday,
Who have temper tantrums in stores and pick at their food,
Who like ghost stories and shove dirty clothes under the bed,
Who never rinse out the tub,
Who squirm in church, and
Who don't like to be hugged or kissed in front of their friends
because it's not "cool."

And we remember the children . . .
Who never get dessert,
Who have no safe blanket to drag behind them,
Who can't find any bread to steal,
Who don't have a room to clean up,
Whose pictures aren't on anyone's dresser,
Who never went to the circus,
Who live in an X-rated world,
Whose smiles can make us cry,
Whose nightmares come in the daytime,
Who will eat anything,
Who have never been to the dentist,
Who aren't spoiled by anybody,
Who go to bed hungry and cry themselves to sleep,
Who *want* to be carried, and for those who *must* be carried,
Who never give up, and for those who never get a second chance,
And we remember the children . . .
Who will grab the hand of anybody kind enough to offer it!

> **Remember, some of us learn from other people's mistakes and the rest of us have to *be* the other people.**

As teachers, it's easy to get this "listening thing" mixed up. Since we observed our teachers doing most of the talking in class . . . and talking . . . and talking . . . we think that's the way it's supposed to be done. Wrong!

Just the facts:

- 80% of a teacher's day is spent communicating, yet it is the one area in which most teachers had the least amount of training. (Emphasis is on public speaking not listening.)

- The most important part of communication is not talking, it's *listening*. But listening is the most ignored skill in education. Students will learn how to listen by seeing you listen.

- Listening is caring. (The word "listen" has the same letters as the word "silent.")

We can touch student's hearts by understanding that only 7% of our communication is with words only. Our tone of voice and volume say more than the words. But what students and others "hear" more than anything is the message we send with our body language.

Imagine the bell just rang at the end of the day. You notice that one particular student is getting his/her books together a little slower than usual. The other students already left and as s/he walks slowly towards the door you casually ask, "Is everything okay?" S/he responds with a lukewarm, "Yes." The fact that they hung around a little longer than usual and their head and eyes are focused on the floor tells you everything is not "okay."

Taking a minute (which you really don't *have* because you need to get to your faculty meeting) to simply tell the student if they ever need anyone to talk to, you're always ready to listen. One simple statement, backed up with actions, can absolutely change the attitude and effort s/he has in your class.

I have participated in group parent-teacher conferences, (been to a "few" yourself, right?), where several teachers are present, and noticed how many times each teacher will share a similar experience such as, "Susie is causing discipline problems," or "Jimmy won't do his work." Every teacher has the same story, except for one teacher. There is usually one teacher who says, "I know this doesn't fit the pattern we see here, but this student works great in my class and never causes any problems."

It's no secret how this happens. Many times this is the highly successful teacher who has connected by encouraging and listening to the student. Because they took the time to let the student know s/he is important, the student and teacher "click" and are on the same wave-length. See a pattern? The student knows the teacher cares so s/he puts more effort in this class.

You will be amazed how you can transform young people and inspire them to think, feel and take action – if you will just make the time to *touch their heart*. (If you are thinking of those few students you don't think you can help change, let me remind you of John Wooden's words, as we previously stated: *"Don't let the things you cannot do interfere with the things you can do!"*)

"One of the most important things a teacher can do is to send the pupil home in the afternoon liking himself just a little better than when he came in the morning."

Ernest Melby

STOP, LOOK & LISTEN!

My mom would say those familiar words to me when I was going to a neighbor's house to play. Powerful words that can help us as adults enjoy life and connect with students.

STOP: Grading papers and completing other paperwork is a very time consuming part of your responsibilities. But if it is interfering with changing student's lives, we need to be conscious of our "busy-ness." While visiting a school, I saw the following sign on a teacher's desk:

"Students aren't an interruption of my work - *they* are the reason I have my job!"

Is that a great thought, or WHAT?! This teacher said it helps keep everything that happens during a typical day in perspective. It's easy to gripe about students, but in reality, would you be employed if they weren't enrolled?

LOOK: Do you see any "body language" messages that tell you how to reach inside your students' hearts? (Even the toughest kid in your class has a heart. Most likely it has been hardened because no one has taken the time to really care. Why not be the teacher that breaks the barriers down and gives students a chance to experience changing their lives?)

LISTEN: After you ask a question, be patient and **<u>really</u> listen**. The best salespeople aren't the "big talkers." It's the ones who listen to what the customer needs. It's the same with highly successfully teachers. What does the student really need? (By the way, you ARE a salesperson. *The most important one in the world.* Beginning with the first day of class you should "sell" your students important ideas such as; why they need to learn what you are going to teach them; how to be responsible; and that they can use their knowledge from your class to be successful!)

Have you ever seen a Chinese bamboo tree? It is one of the most fascinating trees I know of. The first year the tiny seed is planted and is watered, but nothing comes out of the ground. The second year it is watered and nurtured, but nothing comes out of the ground. The same is true for the third and fourth years. But during the fifth year it not only begins growing above the ground, but also grows up to 80 feet in height!

Do you think it only started growing the fifth year? It was growing all the time, it just couldn't be seen. It's the same with nurturing your students' growth. You may be the first person in their life to "plant the seed" of encouragement, and you may not even see the "full-grown tree come out of the ground." But you have played such an instrumental role in their development and success! But first . . .**You must plant the seed!**

This is emphasized in an important article in the *Virginia Journal of Education*, (March 2001), titled, ***"Personal Connection Is Crucial to Learning"*** quoted from "Making Low-Performing Schools A Priority," a publication of the National Education Association:

> *"Many times, what matters most to a student is how his or her teacher demonstrates caring. Learning happens most effectively when students feel like their teacher has a genuine personal connection with them."*

Many days you will try and try and try – unsuccessfully – to reach those "hard-to-reach" students and will leave school feeling as if you aren't making a difference and that this thing of touching students hearts is a bunch of garbage. On those days, (as you know, they seem to come quite often), keep the message of the following story alive in your heart:

I had a very special teacher in high school many years ago whose husband died unexpectedly of a heart attack.

About a week after his death, she shared some of her insight with our class. As the late afternoon sunlight cam streaming in through the classroom windows and the class was nearly over, she moved a few things aside on the edge of her desk and sat down there.

With a gentle look of reflection on her face, she paused and said, "Before class is over, I would like to share with all of you a thought that is unrelated to class, but which I feel is very important. Each of us is put here on earth to learn, share, love, appreciate and give of ourselves.

None of us knows when this fantastic journey experience will end. It can be taken away at any moment. Perhaps this is God's way of telling us that we must make the most out of every single day."

Her eyes beginning to water, she went on, "So I would like you all to make me a promise. From now on, on your way to school, or on your way home, find something beautiful to notice. It might be something you see or a scent or something you hear.

Please look for these things, and cherish them. For, although it may sound trite to some, these things are the "stuff" of life. The little things we are put here on earth to enjoy. The things we often take for granted. We must make it important to notice them, for at any time . . . it can be taken away."

The class was completely quiet. We all picked up our books and filed out of the room silently. That afternoon, I noticed more things on my way home from school than I had the whole semester. Every once in awhile, I think of that teacher and remember what an impression she made on all of us. As we grow older, it is not the things we did that we often regret, but the things we didn't do.

I have learned that the teachers who touched my heart made a much greater impact on my life than the teachers who just tried to teach my mind!

Key Principles for Teaching by Touching Hearts

- *Encouragement and listening* are the "magic keys" to unlock the doors of communication with students.
- The student who treats you the worst is probably the very one who needs your help the most. (They just don't know how to ask you.)
- Treat students as if they are already the person you want them to become and they will usually become that person.
- Successful, caring schools begin with successful, caring teachers.
- Treat students the way you would want a teacher to treat your own child.
- Let students see that you are "human." Begin by letting them see you laugh at yourself when you make mistakes.

Teacher Success Strategy #4
Plan of Action

1. From memory, write Teacher Success Strategy #1:

   ____

2. From memory, write Teacher Success Strategy #2:

   ____

3. From memory, write Teacher Success Strategy #3:

   ____

4. From memory, write Teacher Success Strategy #4:

   ____

Write the name, (or initials), of one student from each of your classes, (or 3 students if you have one class), who it has been difficult for you to touch their heart.

1. ____________________________
2. ____________________________
3. ____________________________
4. ____________________________
5. ____________________________

What do you specifically plan to do to make time and try to "connect" with them?

As suggested in Strategy #1 and #2, what positive tape or book, (your own or from the suggested list in the back), are you using as "input" to keep building your self-esteem?

Odds are, you have been thinking about those "tough kids" as you read this chapter and wonder what specifically you could do to motivate them, right? I hope so, because that's exactly what *Teacher Success Strategy #5* is all about.

Are you "fired up?" If we expect students to be motivated, it starts with us! Get your highlighter ready because now you are going to discover some specific ways to . . .

Motivate Every Student with Enthusiasm and High Expectations!

Let's Go!!

> "Education is not the filling of a pail,
> but the lighting of a fire."
> William Butler Yeats

Teacher Success Strategy #5

Motivate Every Student With Enthusiasm and High Expectations!

Don't you just love experiments? When I took science classes, doing experiments was the best part of class. An experiment was conducted with teachers that literally "knocked the socks off" previously held ideas regarding the impact of teacher expectations on student learning.

"At Oak Elementary School in San Francisco, a group of teachers were told that they were special teachers who were to be part of a special experiment. The researchers said, "Based on a pretest, we have identified 20 percent of your students who are "special." They will be 'spurters' or 'bloomers' and are a designated group of students of whom greater intellectual growth is expected."

The names were actually selected at random, but the teachers were led to believe that the status of being "special" children was based on scores on the pretest, the Harvard Test of Inflected Acquisition.

"As a special reward for your teaching excellence, we are going to tell you this information, but with two conditions:

1. *You must not tell the students that you know that they are special.*
2. *None of us are going to tell the parents that their children are special.*

Thus, we expect and know that you will do extremely well with these special students."

Eight months later, all the students were tested again, and a comparison was made of the designated special students and the undesignated students, as measured by IQ scores. The results showed a significant gain in intellectual growth for the 20 percent who were designated "special."

The administrators brought the teachers in, showed them the growth results of their students, and congratulated them on their spectacular success with their students. The teachers said, "Of course, we had special students to work with. It was easy, and they learned so fast."

The administrators and researcher said, "We'd like to tell you the truth. The so-called "special" children were picked at random. We made no selections based on IQ or aptitude."

"Then it must have been us," said the teachers, "because you said we were special teachers selected to be part of a special experiment." "We need to tell you something else, too," replied the researcher. "All the teachers were involved in this experiment. None of you were designated special over any other teacher."

There was only one experimental variable . . . ***EXPECTATION!"***

(Source: "The First Days of School", Harry K. and Rosemary T. Wong. Rosenthal, Robert, and Lenore Jacobson. (1968) "Pygmalion in the Classroom")

Students will perform only to the level of expectations of the teacher!

Do you remember Teacher Success Strategy No. 1? (In case you're having "one of those days," let me help: **"Unleash Your Personal Power with a Dynamic Self-Image!!"**) One of the most important factors in raising our personal self-esteem is to expect the best of ourselves. This is a prerequisite to expecting the best in our students.

When a student improves their self-esteem they will begin to have more confidence in themselves and expect more of themselves. But it begins with teachers first believing they can get help take students to a higher level.

If you plan on raising students to the next level, you better be on higher ground yourself!

Recently I facilitated a 2-day training session for school superintendents and asked them, "If you could wave a magic wand, what is one of the first things you would change about your teachers?" Seventy percent (70%) of them stated they had so much confidence in teachers doing a great job, but wished the teachers had more confidence in themselves and in their students to raise the performance and achievement bar.

Studies show only 10% of students are intrinsically motivated, (from the inside). All students can use some encouragement, but these students desire to succeed to such an extent, they will do so – in spite of apathetic parents or teachers.

Most likely you also have the opportunity to teach the other 90%, who are average or below average in performance level. Highly successful teachers refuse to complain about the students they are assigned and are determined to assist all students reach their potential.

Flashback . . . back . . . back . . . back . . . to Teacher Success Strategy No. 2. (Change Your Thoughts and You Can Change Your Life!). **Make a choice NOT to focus on the negative information or what other teachers say or how the student has performed in the past.** Focus on what the student *can* accomplish with you this semester or year. Be an encourager and listener and **choose to only expect their best effort – NO EXCEPTIONS!**

Although students may appear to accept or even enjoy classes of teachers with low standards, they actually have more respect for teachers who believe in them enough to demand more, both academically and behaviorally.

In a national survey of 1,300 high school students, (Public Agenda, 1997), teens were asked on questionnaires and in focus groups what they think and want from teachers. Their responses are summarized in the following cluster areas:

Desire for Order: They complained about lax teachers and nonenforced rules. Many feel insulted at the minimal demands placed upon them. They state unequivocally that, "**they would work harder if more were expected of them**."

Desire for Structure: They expressed a desire for "closer monitoring and watchfulness from teachers."

Similarly, when 200 middle school students were surveyed about their most memorable work in school, they repeatedly "equated hard work with success, satisfaction and self-esteem." **They want to be challenged!!!!!** (Wasserstein, 1995)

I have observed that nearly all schools "claim" to hold high expectations. However, in reality, "saying it and doing it" are two different things. I find that most schools have high expectations of only *some* of their students segments, (very few students), and low expectations for most of the other student population.

> "Learning... should be a joy and full of excitement. It is life's greatest adventure: it is an illustrated excursion into the mind of noble and learned men, not a conducted tour through a jail!"
>
> Taylor Caldwell

4 Classic Comments on Teacher Expectations:

"Research clearly establishes that *teacher expectations* do play a significant role in determining how well and how much students learn." (Jerry Bamburg, 1994)

"When *teachers believe in students*, students believe in themselves. When those you respect, (teachers), think you can – YOU think you can!" (James Raffin, 1993)

"The other side of the coin is when students are viewed as lacking in ability or motivation and are *not expected to make significant progress*, they tend to give teachers as little as is expected of them." (Peggy Gonder, 1991)

"One characteristic of a highly-effective teacher is they *refuse to alter their attitudes or expectations for their students* – regardless of the students' race or ethnicity, life experiences and interests, gender, and family wealth and stability." (Barbara & Les Omotani, 1996)

Expectations, as if by magic, come true!

How Teachers Communicate Expectations

Instructions: Self-assess your own communication practices by placing a check mark beside habits you may have unintentionally practiced. Please be honest:

___ 1. Pay less attention to or call on low-expectation students less
___ 2. Seat low-expectation students farther from the teacher
___ 3. Wait less time for low-expectation students to answer questions
___ 4. Criticize low-expectation students *more* frequently for incorrect responses
___ 5. Praise low-expectation students *less* frequently after correct responses
___ 6. Provide low-expectation students with less detailed feedback (written/verbal)
___ 7. Interrupt low-expectation students more frequently
___ 8. Demand less effort from low-expectation students

(Source: Educational Sociology: A Realistic Approach, T. Good and J. Brophy)

In 1997, the New York State Department of Education **put their money $$ where their mouth was**, by deciding to spend $600,000.00 for a teacher training program, to help raise teacher expectations of students. They firmly believe that changing how teachers view their students – *especially their poor-performing students* – is critical to turning around failing schools. **They believe all students can perform at higher levels if they are taught well by teachers who <u>expect</u> them to succeed.** (1997, The New York Times Company)

What YOU Can Do . . .

- Be aware of body language – smile more, have better eye contact
- Move around your classroom
- Allow more time for answers – wait
- Change seating regularly – at least every grading period
- Give low-expectation students more leadership responsibilities
- Stop . . . moans, groans or "You're never right" verbalizations
- Monitor your feelings regularly
- Recognize **effort** – not just top grades

On the first day of school, (or tomorrow, if you are reading this during the school year), tell students what you expect and why you expect their best effort. (Because you believe in them and *know* they will work hard to be successful.)

"70% of all prisoners were told by a teacher and/or parent that, "One of these days you're going to end up in jail!"

Our expectations of students can be life changing . . . for both the teacher and student!

One of my former teachers said to our class on the first day of school, "You've probably heard about me. More students fail my class than pass it and I don't *expect* this group to be any different.

I take pride in the fact that I am the toughest teacher in this school. Last semester only two students received an A and one of them possibly should have received a B+. If you pass this class it's because you worked for your grade because I don't *give* anything."

We agreed with the last statement she made, "She doesn't *give* anything," (including encouragement or help outside the class.) She was telling us **she expected us to fail!!** Talk about a serious self-esteem problem – not us – the teacher. Anyone who has to "fail" students to make her/himself look superior needs to reread Teacher Success Strategy No. 1, regarding improving their self-esteem. **A highly successful teacher finds joy in helping students experience success – not failure!**

"Okay Jerry" you may say, "I will expect their best effort, (this means *really* believing in them), but tell me how I can motivate those apathetic students who put their heads on their desk and sleep. You know you just can't make 'em learn if they don't want to. You can lead a horse to water but can't make him drink."

Good point. Earlier we said, "*You can change another person's behavior/performance by helping them change the picture of him/herself.*" Those apathetic students have a poor picture of themselves and what they can accomplish. Their self-picture may be a result of their parents' lack of success in school and negative attitudes. Or it may be a result of past teachers who focused on their negative behavior and held low expectations of their potential.

> "The most extraordinary thing about a really good teacher is that he or she transcends accepted educational methods."
> Margaret Meade

What an exciting challenge!! YOU could be the very first teacher to daily demonstrate to those apathetic students that you really do care about them – as people and students! That they really do have unlimited potential and talents that the two of you are going to discover together during the year!

Now that you are working to increase the expectations for ALL your students, it's important to know how to motivate them to accomplish more than they think possible. (They don't *know* what is possible because no one has told them or showed them.) So, how much do we know about academic motivation?

Actually, we know a great deal. We know most students begin their formal school experience motivated to learn. (Sometimes in spite of their parents' attitude.) Students have a natural desire to learn and most of them have high expectations for success.

Ever heard of a preschooler being unmotivated? They don't exist. They are propelled by curiosity to explore new things and learn. Even when they fail the first few attempts at something they will keep trying.

Why does this passion for learning for many students decrease to the point of "hating school?" Why do over 25% of all students in the United States quit school before graduating? **They don't believe people care whether they are successful or not**. Show them you DO care about them and expect their best effort every day!

If you have any doubt about this, I suggest you ask a kindergarten teacher in your school or school division if you could drop by sometime to be a "fly on the wall" and observe the anticipation of learning in the eyes and actions of their students. When their teacher asks a question, almost all the children's hands immediately go up accompanied by exclamations of, "I know, I know" or "Pick me, pick me."

For most learners, motivation and optimism begin to diminish with repeated failure. After a few years teachers begin to encounter unmotivated students. Once students begin to believe they cannot be successful, teachers begin to hear comments such as, "I don't want to do this," "I don't care," or "I hate school." Sadly, many teachers begin to accept this "no-care attitude" and lower their expectations of students. **Make a commitment to focus on apathetic students and bring them up to their level of potential instead of them bringing you down to their level of expectations of themselves!**

When you hear students make statements such as these, **don't believe them.** It's easier for them to say they don't care and hate school. If they don't do well, they can save face with their peers because they "didn't try anyway." But if they try and then fail, they lose status and "respect" from their classmates.

As a teacher, <u>your</u> awareness of how students' attitudes and beliefs about learning potential can help reduce student apathy. Can you reach all of them? Probably not. But what about all those with whom you *can* reach and make a difference?

Some of the biggest factors that influence student motivation include: home environment (parents' attitudes), their peer's beliefs about the importance of education, the school setting, classroom environment, (Teacher Success Strategy No. 6 – next chapter - will give you tons of great tips for improving this), and the teacher – YOU!

Please be careful not to fall into the typical "teachers-lounge-talk" of, "You know, you just can't motivate students these days." WRONG! **Every student can be motivated, but not with the same approach** and not in one "giant step." (*Take baby steps.*) Both the apathetic student and the hyperactive student can be motivated to learn.

Understanding Hyperactivity

- A hyperactive parent inquires how his child is doing more than twice a year.
- A hyperactive teacher keeps her/his memos in alphabetical order and files weekly lunch menus chronologically. S/he can tell you what was served on the third Wednesday in October, 1973.
- A hyperactive administrator washes the coffee pot and the cups in the faculty room.
- A hyperactive custodian has never been found.
- A hyperactive student is never absent.

Intrinsic motivation, (self-motivation from the inside), is the result you are striving for, so students will eventually motivate themselves. But many times the *extrinsic motivation*, (from the environment or someone else), is the beginning point of being intrinsically motivated. In other words, when you continually – with daily persistence – offer encouragement to students, they will reach a point where they really feel they can do it on their own, without depending as much on your "motivation."

At the beginning of each school year, how many days does it take you to recognize the students who: speak without permission or talk and joke a lot or are quiet or those who turn in top-quality assignments? Probably just a few days. (In some classes, only a few minutes?)

Applying the principles you learned with the DISC Profiles in Teacher Success Strategy No. 3, can help you motivate students by understanding different approaches will be needed to motivate different students. (This does NOT mean you must spend extra time with each student. You don't *have* any extra time, right?) It *does* mean just like you and your spouse, brothers and sisters, or friends are motivated differently - so are your students motivated differently.

One of the most dynamic ways to motivate students is applying the techniques of DISC. Using DISC allows the teacher to recognize in advance predictable patterns of behavior, work together in harmony and create a "win-win" situation for you to motivate your students.

A Typical Classroom Scenario:
(Source: *Positive Personality Profiles*, Robert A. Rohm, 1993)

The teacher stands up, ready to begin his lesson. Because he is unaware of the different behavior tendencies of his students, (DISC), he is already at a disadvantage in trying to motivate them.

He asks, "Who discovered America?" Ricky – **a high "D"** – bursts out, "Columbus!" The teacher frowns and says, "Ricky, you didn't even raise your hand." Ricky replies, "You asked a question so I thought you wanted an answer."

Again the teacher asks, "All right, who discovered America?" Yvonne – a **high "I"** – shoots her hand up and down, waving her arm side to side, and replies, "Could you give me a hint?" The teacher thinks to himself, "How could this student raise her hand and not know the answer?" (What the teacher, who is unfamiliar with the motivation techniques of DISC doesn't realize is, what Yvonne really heard the teacher say was, *"Would someone like to talk?"*)

The teacher strolls over to Jamie's desk. She has to call on Jamie – the **high "S"** – because Jamie never raises his hand. When she asks Jamie, he replies, "Well, in reading over this material and doing my homework last night, it seems – I may be wrong and I don't want to offend anyone, and if anyone wants to disagree with me that's okay, or if someone wants to take my turn I'll let them because I have probably already taken too long – but I think . . . was it Columbus?" The teacher thinks, "Why is this student so shy and intimidated?"

Then the teacher quizzes Susan – the **high "C"** – and Susan responds, "Who discovered America . . . I'm not sure I understand the question. Do you want me to say Columbus? Before Columbus came, the Indians were here, and before the Indians, the Vikings. So, I'm not sure I understand the question." The teacher is thinking, "Why doesn't someone just answer my simple question?"

The truth is, all the students *are* answering the question – but in their own way.

How You Can Motivate Students Using "DISC":

D – "Determined" Student: Direct/Straightforward, high self-confidence, competitive, can be domineering, strong desire to reach their goals, likes to lead

How to Motivate High "D's": Let them know it's okay to verbalize their feelings in a polite manner – according to your classroom management guidelines, give them responsibilities but let them know when they get out of line, make sure they work "with" you and not against you, let them know it's okay when they don't reach their goals the first time they try

I – "Interactive" Student: Talks and talks and talks . . . outgoing, good sense of humor and personality, wants to be liked, energetic, creative, may be disorganized

How to Motivate High "I's": Put instructions in writing – even something as simple as "turn to page 29" (it helps them get organized), allow them to periodically do something enjoyable –

they are fast-paced and easily bored, listen to them, (after class if necessary) – they enjoy talking and will possibly make their living doing so.

S – "Steady/Softhearted" Student: reserved, may be shy, wants things to stay the same (doesn't like changes, such as classroom rules, procedures, or grading policies) and likes to be a part of the group

How to Motivate High "S's": If changes are necessary explain why, more than any other student – you will need to "seek out" and help them become a part of the class without embarrassing them

C – "Conscientious" Student: consistent, likes to be correct and accurate, will complete assignments exactly as the teacher requested and probably have projects completed before they are due, can be a perfectionist, sets high standards for themselves – sometimes *too* high, doesn't handle criticism very well, takes pride in doing things right – *exactly* right

How to Motivate High "C's": allow them to ask questions – they will have tons of them –without making them feel stupid or laughed at, allow them adequate time to respond to your questions, show respect for their high quality of work by writing a personal note on their paper – they take a lot of pride in doing it "right", if you need help with "numbers", ask this student to assist because it WILL be done correctly

Again, the beauty of the DISC systems is IT WILL REALLY WORK IN YOUR CLASSROOM!! The purpose is not to categorize students in "slots," but recognize that students – like teachers – are different, and therefore, require different approaches to motivation.

In using the classroom scenario above, the teacher who understands and uses DISC to motivate students could have responded accordingly:

High "D" – When Ricky shouted out, "Columbus", the teacher could have said, "That's the right answer, and next time we will also raise our hand, right?"

High "I" – When Yvonne asked, "Could you give me a hint?" the teacher recognizing her as someone who likes to talk, would have actually given a hint to help her get the answer correct, while at the same time would have helped with recognition of others that the High I needs in order to be motivated.

High "S" – Knowing Jamie is a High "S", who does not like to be put on the spot, could have said quietly, "It's not necessary to go into detail, so it will be fine if you will just tell me quickly . . ."

High "C" – Obviously Susan has a need to be correct. That is why she covered every possibility with Columbus, the Indians, and the Vikings. The teacher could have said, "It is so great to have students who really *think* about their answers, but for right now, just give me the bottom line – Who discovered America?"

Sometimes the most meaningful and effective ways of getting results are the most simple. The examples above aren't mind-boggling or major-breakthroughs but simple, motivational techniques that really work!

Apply the motivation principles of DISC with the exciting tips and tools below. Focus on the strategies you CAN apply in your classroom – Don't worry about the ones you *can't* use. If you want to see different results - *motivated students* - you must try different approaches. **Don't just *read* the techniques on the list... DO 'EM!!**

Mammoth Methods of Motivation!

1. BE ENTHUSIASTIC . . . BE ENTHUSIASTIC . . . BE ENTHUSIASTIC!
   Just in case you missed number one and aren't sure what the most effective way of motivating students is – **BE ENTHUSIASTIC!!!!!** If YOU aren't excited about your class, can you really expect your students to be motivated? Regardless of their parents' support and even if you have a "fuddy-duddy" administrator that doesn't care whether it rains or shines during a fire drill, YOU can motivate students! It takes time and lots of effort, but YOU can do it. Believe they can be motivated. Visualize those unmotivated, apathetic students as being excited about learning. Continue treating them as if they are already motivated and they are much more likely to become so. Don't give up on 'em!! You may be the very first teacher who shows you care.

2. BE PREPARED! The Scout's Motto is applicable in motivating students to learn. When you enter your classroom knowing exactly what you want to take place and teach with enthusiasm, even unplanned events and disruptions won't keep you from being successful.

3. Meet one-on-one with students – *especially* those who are apathetic, cause discipline problems, and/or refuse to complete assignments. (In other words, talk to the very students you don't *want* to talk to!)

4. Tell students specifically what they need to do to be successful in your class. Assure them they can do well and you will be there to help them be successful every day.

5. Make expectations high but not so unrealistic very few students will meet your standards. When students know that no matter how hard they work they won't meet your expectations, it has a reverse affect – they will be even less motivated than ever!

6. Give students an opportunity to be successful at the very beginning of the year or semester. Gradually increase the difficulty of the class requirements. This allows students to experience success early.

7. Use a variety of teaching methods, strategies and techniques. Would you be motivated and excited if every chapter assignment was: "Read the chapter, take notes, answer questions at the end of the chapter, take a test" . . . over . . . and over . . .? Neither would I. (Specific

strategies will be included in the next chapter, *"How to Have A Classroom of Excellence and Excitement."*)

8. After taking a test or completing an assignment for a grade, give them feedback as soon as possible. Nothing de-motivates a student faster than to work on a project or study for a test and then the teacher takes several days to grade and return it.

9. Write positive comments on assignments. In addition to marking what was wrong, tell them how to improve. If you can tell they had tried harder, even if their grade hasn't improved . . . tell 'em! **Recognize effort – not just grades!**

10. Find out what their personal interests and hobbies are. **Very Important!** This will help you connect with them as a person. Remember, students really are people and will work harder for teachers they think care about them as a person. **Suggestion:** During the first day or two of a new school year or semester, I always give each student an index card for personal information. After writing the name they would like to be called in class, phone no. and address, I ask them stuff like: name of their favorite dessert; name of their favorite music group, favorite sports team, the food they dislike the most, what would they do first if they won a million dollars, happiest day of their life, and what activities at school and outside school they are involved in. (It really surprises teachers to find out sometimes the "quietest kid in class" is president of their 4-H Club or church youth group.) As you ask each question, be sure to share with the class what YOUR answers are.

For example, my classic answer for the "food I dislike the most" is "brown, mushy bananas that stick on your knife when you try to slice it – yeech!" This helps them see you as a real person - which really surprises some of them. I keep these cards in a file for future use. Unless the class asks you to do so, don't share student responses with the rest of the class. And if you do, don't share *who* gave which answers. This is a great way to let students know you care about them. Wrap a rubber band around the cards and refer to their card before meeting with them individually or in preparation for a parent-teacher conference. Don't bring the card to the meeting, read it prior to your conference. (Parents don't know about your "secret file" and will be impressed that you know their child on a personal basis.)

11. Give them some type of out-of-class assignment on a regular basis. Some classes and grades require more home assignments than others, but every class in every school should require students to be accountable. Also, look for special current events programs on television that relate to your class content. Make it an assignment, possibly write a summary or answer specific questions and discuss it in class the next day. As much as we complain about television, if we look for useful information, we can find it. Think of all the math applications included on programs about prices and our economy. Or science information regarding our environment, technology and research. Social Studies/Government and current events are unlimited. Physical Education and wellness are seen in every sports event. Music of different styles is demonstrated in concerts almost daily. Look for ways to

relate your class to the students' world and you will find plenty of them. Relating your class to the "real world" motivates students. They are able to see "why" they are learning.

12. On the first day of school and periodically during the semester, tell them why you enjoy the particular class or grade you teach and how the information they will learn has helped you in real life. **Sell them on the importance of what they will learn – not just the importance of "getting an education." Be specific.**

13. Write the year of graduation on the board or somewhere in your classroom so students will see it every day. Example: Graduation Date Celebration - June, 2011. If you are a secondary teacher with students of different grade levels, write all graduation dates. For example: Senior Graduation Date Celebration – June 2001, Junior Graduation Date Celebration – June 2002, etc. Seeing their date of graduation every day is a tremendously effective motivating technique. Additionally, I periodically ask the class to say it out loud, as a group, to further plant this goal in their minds.

If you don't know where you're going, you'll probably end up somewhere else!

Instructions: Reread each motivational method listed above and *highlight 3 techniques* you will put into action – **immediately!** Use the specific tools given in Teacher Success Strategy No. 1 – *"Unleash your Personal Power with a Dynamic Self-Image!"* and the tips from Teacher Success Strategy No. 2 – *"Change Your Thinking and You Can Change Your Life!"* to help you build your own confidence and enthusiasm. Whatever you do – **Be Enthusiastic!** Write the 3 Motivational Methods you highlighted and will use below:

1. ______________________________
2. ______________________________
3. ______________________________

Motivating students will require a consistent plan and a caring attitude but the results can be "life-changing" . . . both for your students and YOU!

I challenge you to possibly be the first teacher to make a real difference in the lives of those "average or low-performing students". Arrive at class prepared each day, expecting every student's best effort and I promise you will begin to see dramatic changes in your students and yourself. It won't happen overnight, or even in one grading period, but make a decision and a commitment not to give up on anyone and <u>it will happen</u> – sooner than you think!

Key Principles of Motivating Every Student with Enthusiasm and High Expectations!

- Expect and accept only the best effort of ALL students!
- Be enthusiastic and prepared . . . every day!
- Apply the motivational principles of DISC!
- Never, never, never, never . . . give up on any student!

Teacher Success Strategy #5
Plan of Action

1. Write, from memory, Teacher Success Strategy #1:

   ____

2. Write, from memory, Teacher Success Strategy #2:

   ____

3. Write, from memory, Teacher Success Strategy #3:

   ____

4. Write, from memory, Teacher Success Strategy #4:

   ____

5. Write, from memory, Teacher Success Strategy #5:

   ____

6. Write the names, or initials, of 3 students you will individually begin to mentor as part of implementing your Motivational Plan of Action . . . NOW!
   1.__________ 2.__________ 3.__________

7. What tape or book are you using for your own personal inspiration? ________________________________

Only one more strategy before you begin your **10-Day Personal Plan of Action!** We're almost there. Our last strategy, *"Create a Classroom of Excellence and Excitement!,"* is the most dynamic because you are going to combine Teacher Success Strategies #1-#5 to get students excited about learning and life!

I just want to know . . .
ARE YOU READY?

I <u>KNOW</u> YOU ARE!
LET'S GO!

> "Always teach as though you were teaching your own children."
>
> Anonymous

Teacher Success Strategy #6

Create a Dynamic Classroom of Excellence and Excitement!

As a first year teacher, I had heard all the veteran teachers talk about a nightmare experience called "being observed." Throughout the fall no one had visited my classroom and since this was the last day of school before Christmas break, I thought I had "made it" until the first of the year. Now I understand that's when teachers get into trouble – when they begin to think.

As I stood in front of my General Business class, sharing the important points of Creative Advertising Methods, it happened . . . Mr. Evaluator Administrator entered my world. (Note: His real name has been changed to protect the innocent – ME.) As he walked to an empty desk in the back of the room, he immediately began writing in his big, yellow, "How many things Jerry did wrong" legal pad. I am a very positive person, but must admit I did not think it was a good sign when he started writing before he even sat down!

Teachers had described Mr. Evaluator Administrator as the "Candid Camera Man," because "sometime, somewhere, when you least expect it" he would throw your classroom door open as if to say, "Smile –Today is YOUR day to be evaluated! You DO have your lesson plans prepared for the next 17 years, don't you?"

Now you must grasp the full picture of this situation. First, the class was called General Business. To this day, I firmly believe the Guidance Department went through the entire school enrollment and said, "Let's see, she missed 74 days of school last year and probably won't graduate, put her in General Business." "He has been in a Juvenile Detention Home 14 times and will possibly end up in jail, so put him in General Business." Possibly a little exaggeration, but you get the picture of the kind of students assigned to my class. Four classes of, let's see . . . students who were . . . uh, well . . . pretty . . . GENERAL! Not exactly motivated to become great pillars of the community.

Needless to say, in order to motivate them to learn, I would use practically any teaching strategy that was family appropriate, moral, and legal. So, the day Mr. Evaluator Administrator blessed us with his presence, I was doing what any dedicated teacher would be doing – TEACHING! No last day parties during instructional time for me. (Actually, I had my Christmas parties three days earlier.)

There was only one reason I could understand why he wasted no time in beginning to fill in 37 pages in his legal pad: While I was teaching . . . **I was standing on top of my desk, wearing a complete Santa Claus suit – including beard, hat and boots!!** Here I was, a first year teacher, my first observation and evaluation, and I'm standing in front of my class dressed up like Santa Claus. You're probably wondering what my first reaction was. I can assure you it was ***not,*** "Ho Ho Ho." I did exactly what you would probably do. I immediately looked down at the desk to see if there was a secret trap door I could fall through. When I realized there wasn't, I had no choice but to continue teaching as if this was a "normal" situation.

As I continued teaching, while standing on the top of my desk, my next thoughts were, "Okay, Jerry. Try to be cool about this, even though this is probably the last day of teaching in this school division, or anywhere. And even though you've spent a lot of time and money preparing to be a teacher, you might begin considering what your *second* career choice would be."

Somehow I made it through the class. And except for one student interrupting me by asking loudly enough for the class across the hall to hear him, "Mr. King, you're not going to give us homework today just to impress that old man in the back row, are you?" it went about as well as could be expected.

The bell rang and as the students were leaving I jumped down from the desk. As I was taking off my beard and Santa hat he approached me and said, "Could you come by my office for a few minutes after school today to discuss your evaluation?" Something evil inside me wanted to reply, "Actually, Mr. Little Larry Legal Pad, I have already made plans to be home by 4:00 so I can watch a rerun of the *Andy Griffith Show*. The episode today is the one where both Barney and Otis lock themselves in the jail cell." But, I resisted and very hypocritically said, "I'll be glad to." Which, of course, was a complete lie. Teachers are "glad to" leave most in-service training sessions early, and we are "glad to" help with the paperwork needed to transfer the student who has been the biggest discipline problem in our class to another school, but we are NOT "glad to" attend a meeting regarding our evaluation after we have taught a class while dressed as Santa Claus!

The shock of my new teaching career and something that profoundly affected my teaching in a positive way throughout the following years occurred at that meeting. Instead of telling me how crazy I was for trying a unique teaching strategy, (and that I needed to clean out my desk and turn in my room key), he said to me, "You did something today that many teachers finish their teaching career and never do, *you brought your unique personality inside the classroom and used it to reach a very hard-to-reach group of students. Continue to "be yourself" and use creative teaching strategies to* ***create a classroom of excellence and excitement***."

To this day, I don't know if his description of me as being "unique" meant he thought I was a crazy, loony-tune teacher. But I *do* know his encouragement was what I needed to hear. Be willing to step outside your comfort zone and use a variety of "terrific teaching tools and techniques."

This chapter includes a "ton of terrific tips and techniques" from highly effective teachers that can help you **Create A Classroom of Excellence and Excitement.** As I emphasized throughout this book, don't just read it - "do" it. Use your highlighter and/or ink pen as you read and mark the techniques you feel fit your style and personality. Don't be afraid to step out of your comfort zone and try things you haven't tried before.

If someone told you the exact steps necessary and how to become a successful, highly successful millionaire within a year, would you listen and do what they say – assuming it was legal and moral? Let's begin our final strategy of becoming a highly successful teacher by looking at what the most effective ways of teaching are.

Remember: If you are not satisfied with your current results – low-performing, apathetic, or discipline-challenging students – you MUST change what you are doing!! If you don't change what you are doing in your classroom, don't expect your results to change. It won't happen! ("*If you keep doing what you've been doing, you're gonna keep getting what you've got!*") What are the most effective teaching methods?

Teaching Methods and Average Retention Rate

- Lecture – 5%
- Reading – 10%
- Audiovisuals – 20%
- Demonstrate – 30%
- Discussion Groups – 50%
- Practice by doing – 75%
- Students involved in teaching others – 80%

Based on the list above, please write the *least* effective way of helping students retain information: ______________________.
(If you wrote "Lecture" you are correct.)

Please write what method you think is most widely used by teachers: _____________.
(If you wrote "Lecture" again, you are "two for two.")

Students forget 90% of what they hear during a lecture within 10 days!

If teachers were truly interested in improving learning and test scores, why would they use the method that is **least effective** for learning? There are many reasons, but one of the leading factors is we "tend to teach the way we have been taught." If you and I were taught by teachers who mainly used the lecture method, it is only natural we would follow in their footsteps. There is only one problem. Just because *they* used the lecture method most of the time doesn't mean it was the best. Highly successful teachers are willing to try things they sometimes don't feel "comfortable" trying, such as using a variety of teaching techniques to help students learn as quickly as possible and to improve their long-term retention rate. Why is it important to use a variety of teaching techniques?

The average attention span of a high school student is only 12-14 minutes!

Obviously, we can "cover" the material using only the lecture method, but for most of the class time we have "lost 'em." One teacher told me, **"Teachers *covering* it and students *containing* it, may be two completely different things."**

2 Foundation Principles of Highly-Effective Teachers need to be understood *before* we discover specific classroom strategies. In order for you to apply the specific teaching strategies from this chapter in your classroom, highlight the important points of these two principles:

- *Master the Principles of Effective Classroom Management*
- *Apply the Principles of Accelerated Leaning*

Principles of Effective Classroom Management:

How much time during a typical day do you think you spend dealing with students who are disrupting your teaching (discipline situations), and doing non-teaching chores such as calling roll and returning papers? *Research says teachers spend an average of 1/3 of their time in class with such activities!!* Think about how much more teaching and learning could take place by simply managing our class more effectively.

I highly recommend a book written by Harry K. and Rosemary T. Wong, *"The First Days of School."* It contains this useful information plus many additional suggestions on becoming a highly successful teacher.

The effectiveness of your classroom – excellence and excitement – depends on how well you manage your classroom. **You can have the best lesson plans prepared and be enthusiastic about what you plan to do each day, but if your class is "out-of-control," you will get very little accomplished.** Proper management of your classroom is necessary before anyone can teach anything effectively.

"The #1 factor governing student learning is <u>classroom management</u>!"

(Wong, Dec. 1993, *"What Helps Students Learn"*. Ed. Leadership, pp 74-79)

If you sincerely want to have *a classroom of excellence and excitement*, practice classroom management procedures - beginning the first day of school. You need to practice and rehearse the procedures you want your students to follow – some of them over and over until they get it right. You probably have participated in a "few" fire drills at your school, right? The reason you practice what to do in case of a fire BEFORE a fire actually occurs is so you will know ahead of time what you should do. The same principle applies to the need for you to rehearse your desired classroom procedures – beginning the first day of school – BEFORE discipline problems occur.

First Day of School:

1. Prepare a seating chart before students arrive. Either have each class diagrammed with names of students at your desired seating place, with the overhead turned on as they arrive, or hold a master seating chart and show them to their assigned seat. (Each class diagram will take you about 5 minutes to prepare and will save you HOURS in correcting possible discipline situations. "Pay a little now or a lot later.") Many elementary teachers place a creative nameplate on each student's desk, but if you have more than one class you should consider one of the methods above – or even better – be creative and come up with your

own way of doing it! Older students do not like being told where to sit, but using a seating chart will help you learn student's names, check attendance without "calling roll" and separate possible discipline problems. Unless you have a very unusual situation - **Do not allow students to "sit where they want to."** Also, change their seating arrangements periodically.

2. Greet students as they arrive and have a short assignment on the board so they may immediately begin working. It may be something as simple as filling out a form. (Note: I write three things in a special place on the board – every day: 1. A Positive Power Thought for the Day, 2. A trivia question (that relates to the subject content), 3. A short class assignment)

3. When introducing rules: give them a written copy, have the rules and consequences posted in the room, and ask students to repeat them out loud. Repetition enhances memory. Try not to have more than 3-5 *classroom* rules. These rules are in addition to school or school district rules and include areas such as respect for other students, etc.

4. **Important!** *Procedures and routines must be rehearsed.* Explain exactly how you want certain things done. Be very specific. For example, many teachers allow their students to turn in their test as they finish. Every time a student gets out of his/her seat to walk to the desk it disrupts and distract other students who are trying to finish their tests. As more students finish, the noise level tends to increase. I found when I enforced the rule of "absolutely no talking until I take up all tests after everyone is finished or you will

receive a "0" and allowed them to work on something else when they finished, everyone stayed quiet until the last person finished. This was my procedure and we literally rehearsed it. By the way, another procedure is exactly how you want them to pass in their papers.

Possible Additional Procedures and Routines:

- Taking roll
- Absences and tardies
- Asking questions/need help
- Being excused from the classroom
- Fire Drills
- Taking tests
- Beginning of class
- Watching an audio-visual
- Getting into small groups

Don't take for granted they automatically know how you want things done. Explaining and rehearsing will save you a lot of time and headaches. After teaching our classroom management procedures, the second important prerequisite to having a classroom of excellence and excitement is to apply the basic principles of Accelerated Learning.

There are many knowledgeable authors in this area, but I highly recommend a book written by Dave Meier, *"The Accelerated Learning Handbook."* In addition to these guidelines, it contains numerous ways to help you achieve a learning environment where students enjoy learning and you can be the highly successful teacher you were meant to be.

> "Teachers, students, parents, and communities should stick together. Remember; the banana gets skinned only when it gets away from the bunch."

Principles of Accelerated Learning:

Accelerated Learning has one aim: **To get results!** When you apply these principles, your students will learn faster, remember it longer and enjoy learning more. Accelerated Learning's approach is, "*Do what works and keep searching for what works better!*" There is a place for enjoyment and a place for seriousness. Teachers and students need both. Suggestion: Highlight the basic principles of areas in which you need to improve:

Accelerated Learning Basics

- Approach every teaching strategy with an open mind
- Get out of the "*I-tell, you-listen*" format. (Commonly known as the "*Pour and snore*" technique!)
- Students learn better in a relaxed and stimulating environment
- Learning is not a spectator sport – watching the teacher perform. Students learn better when they are totally, actively involved.
- All good learning will include social aspects (Collaboration)
- Students learn best when there are a variety of learning options

- Students learn best when they see *how* the information will be used (Contextual Learning)
- Students learn best when learning involves both mind and the body – **MOVE**!
- Feelings and emotions affect learning. (Negative feelings inhibit learning, positive feelings accelerate learning. Refer to Teacher Success Strategy #4; "*Touch Their Hearts Before You Teach Their Minds.*")

Don't just sit there . . . DO SOMETHING!!

Can you imagine a young child sitting for hours while the teacher "lectures" to her/him? And yet, knowing that a high school student's attention span is 12-14 minutes long, (elementary students even less), we expect them to be at peak learning capacity without getting out of their seats for 45-90 minutes. It's absurd! Learning is hampered when we separate the body and the mind. The mind falls asleep when there is no chance for some kind of physical involvement. ***Moving allows blood to flow to the brain and helps us learn faster!*** That 15-20 second stand-and-stretch break that so many teachers "just don't have time for" is probably the most important activity during class. It helps students refocus on what we want them to learn.

Want to get 'em fired up? Include all four phases of learning in every class:

1. ***Preparation*** – arouse student's interest and give them positive feelings about what you are going to teach. For

example, how they will be able to use their knowledge in the real world.

2. ***Presentation*** **-** making the learning material interesting – use a *variety* of teaching strategies (as opposed to mostly "lecture")

3. ***Practice*** – help students incorporate the new knowledge – hands on, problem solving, teams, etc.

4. ***Performance*** **-** help students apply and extend their knowledge – go past the classroom experience

Highly effective teachers understand and use the **"SAVI"** principle, the core of Accelerated Learning, as often as possible:

S = Somatic – Learning by moving and doing
A = Auditory – Learn by talking and hearing
V = Visual – Learn by observing and with mental pictures
I = Intellectual – Learning by problem solving

Bust Out of Your Comfort Zone with Accelerated Learning!

So, what's the difference between a highly effective teacher, who uses the result-proven teaching strategies of Accelerated Learning and a teacher who just "covers the material?"

Traditional Learning	*Accelerated Learning*
Rigid	Flexible
Controlling	Nurturing
Mental (cognitive)	Mental/Physical/Emotional
Time-Based	Results-Based
Serious/Somber	Joyful

Did you read that last one? The difference between being serious and somber and being joyful! Jerry, you mean it's okay to "enjoy" teaching and learning?

The days of "Don't Smile Until Christmas" for teachers went out with the horse and buggy!

A few years ago I attended a teacher in-service training and the speaker proceeded to emphasize that school was not a place for fun and laughter. This statement was made at the beginning of an all-day, six-hour training session where he told 43 funny one-liners, jokes or funny stories! (Yes, because I disagreed so much with him about the place of "joy" in school, I actually counted them.) If humor wasn't important in teaching and learning, why did he use it all day to keep our attention? Apparently, it's a great technique for teaching teachers but not for teaching students!

Think about the last speaker or minister you heard. What was their "main point?" If you're like most people, we've forgotten it by the time we return home – many times before we leave the parking lot! Now, see if you can remember a funny story *that related to their "main point."* Odds are, if we remember anything about what someone says, we remember the humor. Should all teaching and classes be loaded with humor? Of course not. But teachers who don't include an interesting story or humor to help students retain knowledge are leaving out a very effective way of improving long-term-retention and improving test scores!

There is a time and a place for everything. Creativity, joy and humor help teachers connect with students. I'm not referring to telling jokes or being a "funny person." I'm referring to creating an atmosphere where students do not feel threatened or embarrassed if they make a mistake or say something wrong.

In addition to *"The 6 Dynamic Strategies of Highly Successful Teachers,"* one of the most requested in-service programs I am asked to facilitate at schools and conferences is, *"Learning 'n Laughing."* I include specific creative teaching techniques teachers can use and emphasize:

Using joy, creativity and humor in the classroom is NOT:

- Telling jokes
- Losing control of classroom discipline
- Teaching less subject matter
- Adding preparation time to lesson plans

Benefits of using joy, humor and creativity:

- Builds rapport between students and the teacher
- Maintains a high attention level
- Increases long-term retention
- Promotes divergent thinking
- Enhances self-esteem
- Creates a positive learning environment

Always be yourself, but don't be afraid to allow students to see the "human side" of you. Most humans laugh every now and then. If nothing else, let them see you laugh at yourself *when* you make a mistake. Again, I didn't say IF you make a mistake, I said WHEN you make a mistake. Their respect for you will vastly improve when you admit mistakes and laugh at yourself – when it is appropriate. (Reminder: Teacher Success Strategy #4: *"Touch Their Hearts Before Teaching Their Minds."*)

You have the "meat 'n tators" of highly successful teaching, now it's time for dessert!"

My favorite part of the meal. You are now familiar with the basic principles of successful classroom management and Accelerated Learning techniques. It's time to **apply these principles to <u>your</u> classroom!**

A resource book *for* highly successful teachers should include specific teaching tools being used *by* highly successful teachers and educators. The following list is a result of personal interviews with highly successful educators who share their dynamic classroom teaching strategies. These exciting techniques really work! Don't let the ones that *don't* apply to your current teaching situation block out the ones you *can* use. Look for and highlight the ones you *will* use. Step out of your comfort zone and - DO IT! Using these tools and techniques will result in YOU . . .***Creating a Classroom of Excellence and Excitement!***

Classroom Strategies for Highly Successful Teachers

Note: As you read the following strategies and suggestions by highly successful classroom teachers, look for ways to make them work in your classroom. With a little imagination and a few changes, many of these can be used at every level and in many classes.

"Use a karoke machine (or cd/tape player) and play oldies. Use a camera. If you have access to a digital camera, children can have their own disk. I use a digital camera to illustrate action. After the pictures have been taken, the students print them and write about the picture. Photos can be incorporated into holiday cards for parents, also. Hold class meetings and let students air their frustrations and learn to solve problems. Allowing them to have a part in classroom rules and activities teaches them about the democratic process and gives them ownership into their classroom as a community." (Music sets a positive tone in class, (when appropriate) and also between classes, as students are leaving and/arriving. Students are motivated to work for teachers who care enough to display pictures of their students in the classroom.)

Judy Berry

"It is important for a teacher to like his/her students and the subject matter being taught. Students experience a personal reaction to real life when we do projects involving the economy. One of the classroom projects we do is use cardboard to construct buildings and build a town. (Businesses, public buildings etc.) Before the student's very eyes, they see how when factories lay people off, businesses possibly close and homes are foreclosed. But, in the upswing economy there is hope for more demand for new houses and businesses." (Think of the practical writing, reading and speaking experiences you could create from this or another "building" project in your classroom. Build a theatre, build a math or science model, etc.)

Bill Holloway

"Don't be afraid to try simple ideas and hands-on activities with high school students. When I'm having a frustrating day with a student, I try to remember something about that student I appreciate or like. This helps me keep my perspective." (As stated earlier, these and other dynamic suggestions relate to <u>all</u> grade levels.)

Susanne Dana

"The one thing that all of my students remember and return to tell me about are Jack Tales by Richard Chase. One day a week I paraphrase and put as much expression as possible into my reading. Also, one day a week my class *works* with Legos – not *play* with Legos. Great to divide the class in pairs and do creative thinking projects. They make everything from compactors to carnival rides and learn much more in this setting than they do from just using the book." (Students are never too old to be read to. If we want students to read more, guess who they need to see and hear read?)

Larry Dalton

"A couple of classroom management strategies I use include: I require students to sign in. I hold anyone tardy (unexcused) after the dismissal bell. I have NEVER had to refer a student to the office because they hate being held after class and I have a written record of their tardy (in their own handwriting); Also, I let students get up and turn in assignments rather than pass it forward. I have found this eliminates restlessness. A few teaching strategies I use include: Give spontaneous notebook quizzes that are designed to measure note-taking and organizational skills; Dress as favorite character – it forces research and investigation; We have Internet Scavenger Hunts. They take some time to plan but are terrific for lower-level learners. The possibilities are endless."

Nancy Muncie

"I make an effort to keep kids out of a *cognition coma.* It all started when I was a student teacher. We were studying ancient Egypt and I decided to mummify a chicken. We used a clear jar so the kids could watch the change. In the mean time, we had an archeological dig in the woods outside the school. The students found "ancient" Egyptian relics, bones and other things I had planted under leaves and sticks. Two months later the chicken was mummified and the kids were still talking about Egypt. Today I use a technique I call *"contagious cognition."* We don't "study" anything in my class. Instead, the kids get to "be" people, such as judges, lawyers, and even teachers. "Being" civics beats "studying" it. I thank parents and tell them I couldn't do what I do without the help of their child. *Teaching is a team effort. I'm the coach.*" (Think of ways you can get students actively involved in learning. The more active they are, the more motivated they will be and the longer they will remember it.)

John Gleason

"The most important thing a teacher can do is be a facilitator to the students. The student should not perceive the teacher as "know all, holder of knowledge." Foster a climate of "community" in the classroom that works to support one another's learning. This community can only be built and supported by mutual trust and respect."

Donna Keck

"I often put lists or sequences to music. For example, to learn how light passes through different parts of the eye, we acted out each motion and as a class chanted: "Cornea-Pupil-Iris-Lens-Retina-Optic Nerve," etc. We use tunes everyone is familiar with. 86 students took the test on the eye and 83 did it correctly without a hitch! (I'm pretty sure the other 3 were absent the day we acted it out.) The best part is hearing all of the humming during the test! I love it!" (Students love music. If you are not musically inclined, odds are most of your students will amaze you with their ability of putting information they need to memorize to either nursery rhyme songs or "appropriate" rap, rock or country tunes.)

Michael Lester

"Students test which dishwashing detergent blows the biggest bubbles. Test by dipping a straw in the solution and blowing a bubble on a wet surface. Results can be written and or graphed. Have students observe something and keep a diary about how things change. For example, Moon Diaries. As a writing process use: **P. O. W. E. R.** (Plan, Organize, Write, Evaluate, Revise) Also, we play a learning game called SURVIVAL, using life cards (fire, disease, animals, etc.)" (Tests and experiments are not just used in science class. Think of ways to get students involved in their world and relate it to your subject.)

Tammy Bowers

"A good sense of humor and lots of laughter makes for a warm, inviting classroom environment. Teacher expectations for behavior and academic success must be clearly understood. Interactive units are always a hit. I use every opportunity possible to give the students situations to experience real life. Assign groups to work together as much as possible by mixing abilities and personalities. Assign each person a job (note taker, leader, artist, monitor etc.) No matter what the subject, effective teaching involves consistency, organization, creativity, a sense of humor and above all fairness and mutual respect."

Mary Blake

"I believe the following components will help teachers prepare students to become more successful in the classroom, on standardized tests and in the biggest test of all – life.
Humanize Instruction: Believe that all students can learn. Listen to all students. Make students feel welcome. Be empathetic to diverse cultures, social backgrounds and ability levels. *Apply Effective Teaching Strategies:* Use auditory, visual and kinesthetic interactions daily. Do not assume students understand the concepts or information. *Efficient Planning:* Assess performance of students and ourselves daily. Eliminate busy work! I use quizzes daily. The emphasis is placed on *learning* not *failing*. My goal is to teach students to succeed; Classroom management has to be structured. Review, introduce and relate information; to save time and confusion when a student returns after being absent, I provide each student with their personal manila folder at the beginning of

the year. Any papers I return or work we do while they are absent is placed in their folder. When they return, they know exactly where their make-up work is with no interruption of class; I teach and review vocabulary by placing the most important terms on the walls, using various colors of construction paper. It brightens the room and wherever the student looks they observe vocabulary. To help remind students and to keep myself on track I make badges. Don't laugh – it works! Some of the messages I have used include: "**S.O.L.** – **S**uccessful **O**pportunities for **L**earning" and "Active Teaching Facilitates Active Learning." And remember: Every *day is game day!*

Charles Hicks

My personal summary of the exciting teaching **strategies** above is:

S top
T eaching
R eruns
A nd
T hrust
E nthusiastic/**E**ducational
G enius
I nto
E very
S ubject

"And in closing . . ."

I once shared with my pastor that I truly believe ministers learn that "magic line" in seminary as a technique for "waking up" the congregation during a sermon. Just when everyone finds a comfortable position in the pew we hear, " . . .*and in closing* . . ." Everyone sits up, gets their car keys, then he continues to speak for another 20-25 minutes.

My use of this familiar phrase is not a "false alarm," because we are nearing the end of this part of our success journey together.

Because you made a commitment to read and "do" the strategies in this book, you are already experiencing positive changes in your life. YOU possess all the necessary character traits needed to become a highly successful person and teacher.

I would like to share a profound story I heard a few years ago because it had a life-changing impact on my success journey. It is a true story, titled "*Acres of Diamonds.*"

A farmer in Africa heard about other farmers getting rich by finding diamonds in rivers and became so excited he sold his farm to go look for these *Acres of Diamonds*. He spent the next thirty years traveling, looking unsuccessfully for the diamonds. He eventually became so discouraged he threw himself in a river and drowned.

Meanwhile back at the ranch, or in this case the farm, the man who bought his farm was crossing a stream and saw a large, sparkling stone in the water. He picked it up, admired it, and put it on his fireplace mantle where it served as a great conversation piece for visitors in his home. Several weeks later, a visitor asked him if he knew what he had found. The farmer told him he thought it was a piece of crystal because even though the other stones weren't as large as this one, his riverbed was full of such stones.

The farm the farmer had sold to this man turned out to be the most productive diamond mine on the African continent!

Important lessons teachers can learn:

- To be a winner in life and in the classroom, we must *expect* to win and *prepare* to win. The farmer didn't take the time or energy to learn what a diamond even looked like.
- We should first look at what we already have, before looking in other places or at other people.
- Each of us is standing – right now – in our own *Acres of Diamonds*. Some of your greatest "riches" in life are sitting in desks every day in your classroom, waiting for you to guide and lead them to success. All we need to do is explore these riches and seek to develop these "rough diamonds," instead of looking elsewhere.
- Your mind is one of your greatest resources. In order to experience a richer, more meaningful life, **you must be willing to change**. To be a "diamond miner" you have to break away from the crowd. To become a highly successful teacher, you cannot be satisfied with being "average."
- Opportunities for success are all around you. Look at your world – your family and students – with new eyes!

You are living and working in *Acres of Diamonds*! Understand you have everything you need within yourself to become the highly successful teacher and person you were created to be. Begin today! Put your plan of action in gear to reach your dreams! And whatever you do:
Don't ever . . .ever . . .ever . . .ever . . .ever . . .quit!

<u>YOU</u> CAN DO IT!

"I Am A Teacher"

I am a teacher!

I was born the first moment that a question leaped from the mouth of a child.

The names of those who have practiced my profession ring like a hall of fame for humanity . . . Booker T. Washington, Buddha, Confucius, Ralph Waldo Emerson, Moses and Jesus.

I have wept for joy at the weddings of former students, laughed with glee at the birth of their children and stood with head bowed in grief and confusion by graves dug too soon for bodies far too young.

Throughout the course of a day I have been called upon to be an actor, friend, nurse and doctor, coach, finder of lost articles, money lender, taxi driver, psychologist, substitute parent, salesman, politician and keeper of the faith.

Despite the maps, charts, formulas, verbs, stories and books, I have really had nothing to teach, for my students really have only themselves to learn, and I know it takes the whole world to tell who you are.

I am a paradox. I speak loudest when I listen the most. My greatest gifts are in what I am willing to appreciatively receive from my students.

Material wealth is not one of my goals, but I am a full-time treasure seeker in my quest for new opportunities for my students to use their talents and in my constant search for those talents that sometimes lie buried in self-defeat.

I am the most fortunate of all who labor.

A doctor is allowed to usher life into the world in one magic moment. I am allowed to see that life is reborn each day with new questions, ideas and friendships.

An architect knows that if he builds with care, his structure may stand for centuries.

A teacher knows that if he builds with love and truth, what he builds will last forever.

I am a warrior, daily doing battle against peer pressure, negativity, fear, conformity, prejudice, ignorance and apathy. But I love great allies: Intelligence, Curiosity, Parental Support, Individuality, Creativity, Faith, Love and Laughter all rush to my banner with indomitable support.

And whom do I have to thank for this wonderful life I am so fortunate to experience, but you the public, the parents. For you have done me the great honor to entrust to me your greatest contribution to eternity – your children.

And so I have a past that is rich in memories. I have a present that is challenging, adventurous and fun because I am allowed to spend my days with the future.

I am a teacher . . . and I thank God for it every day!

John W. Schlatter

"I touch the future. I teach."
Christa McAuliffe, American Teacher

SCHOOL BUS
35

Excellent!

10-Day Personal Power Plan of Action for Highly Successful Teachers!

(To be completed only after learning Teacher Success Strategies 1 – 6)

This is your personal plan for applying "The 6 Dynamic Strategies of Highly Successful Teachers" in your life! Make a commitment to complete your *10-Day Personal Power Plan of Action* EVERY DAY before you begin your teaching responsibilities. Don't *have* the time? I encourage you to *make* the time! This is the most important 5 minutes of your day. Highly successful teachers know they must be positively mentally prepared for the challenges of their teaching day. Don't let anything take priority over completing this action plan each day.

"*Home Play*"

(You already have too much homework.)

In addition to completing your "*10-Day Personal Power Plan of Action*" each morning, I highly recommend you read or listen to one of the books/books-on-tape listed below. Use "Automobile University" to stay motivated. Turn your radio off and play an inspirational tape while traveling to and from school each day. It WILL make a positive difference in your life!

Inspirational Audio/Book Resources

- ***Awaken the Giant Within*** **– Anthony Robbins**
- ***Don't Sweat the Small Stuff*** **– Richard Carlson**
- ***Live Your Dreams*** **– Les Brown**
- ***Over the Top*** **– Zig Ziglar**
- ***Success Through A Positive Mental Attitude*** **– Napoleon Hill**
- ***Success and the Self-Image*** **– Zig Ziglar**
- ***The Winning Attitude*** **– John C. Maxwell**

My Personal Power Plan of Action

Day One

Today's Date: ______________________

Positive Affirmation Thought for the Day: (Write on an index card and carry with you.)

**"Every day in every way,
I'm getting better and better."**

Lighter Side of Teaching:

"You Might Be a Teacher If . . ."

- You suggest to a difficult parent that they really should look into home schooling or charter schools.
- You want to slap the next person who says, "Must be nice to work from 8 to 3 and have summers off."
- When out in public, you feel the urge to talk to strange children and correct their behavior.
- You stand on your front porch and instruct the neighbor's children to, "Walk!"

- You believe "extremely annoying" should have it's own box on the report card.
- You give your spouse "the look" when misbehaving.
- Putting "all A's" on the report card would be so much easier.
- You've ever had your profession slammed by someone who would never dream of doing your job.
- You think caffeine should be available in IV form.

Inspiration/Motivation:

"The Sculptor's Attitude of Teaching"

I woke up early today, excited about all I get to do before the clock strikes midnight. I have responsibilities to fulfill at home and at school today. **I am important because I am a teacher**. I can choose what kind of day I am going to have. I can complain because the weather is rainy or . . . I can be thankful the grass is getting watered for free.

Today I can grumble about my health or . . . I can rejoice that I am alive. Today I can gripe about my "problem" students or . . .I can enthusiastically try to open their minds and learn about life. Today I can whine because I have to go to work or . . . I can shout for joy because I have the most important job in the world – *teaching young people!*

Today stretches ahead of me, waiting to be shaped. And here I am, the sculptor who gets to do the shaping. What today will be like is up to me. I get to choose what kind of day I will have.

I CHOOSE TO HAVE A GREAT DAY!!

1. **Attitude of Gratitude**: Write the name of one person and something you are grateful for today.

   ____

2. Write the name (or initials) of one person you will listen to and encourage today:

   ____

Day Two

Today's Date: ____________________

Excellent!

Positive Affirmation Thought for the Day: (Write on an index card and carry with you.)

"People don't care how much I know, until they know how much I care."

Lighter Side of Teaching:

"Murphy's Law for Teachers"

- Good students always move away.
- New students come from schools that do not teach anything.
- The shorter the working time, the more likely the copy machine to malfunction.
- The problem child will always be an administrator's or school board member's son or daughter.
- Students who improve are credited with working harder. But if students begin to do poorly, it is the teacher's fault.
- Clocks will run more quickly during free time or planning periods.
- The length of a meeting will be directly proportional to the boredom the speaker produces.
- On test day, at least 25% of the class will be absent.
- A disaster will occur when visitors are in the classroom.

Inspiration/Motivation:

"An Important Lesson to Learn About Life"

During my second semester of college, our professor gave us a pop-quiz. I was a conscientious student and had breezed through the questions, until I read the last one: "What is the first name of the person who cleans our building?"

Surely this was some kind of a joke. I had seen the woman several times. She was tall, dark-haired and in her 50's, but how would I know her name? I handed in my paper, leaving the last question blank. Just before class ended, one student asked if the last question would count toward our quiz grade.

"Absolutely" said our professor. "In your careers, you will meet many people. All are significant. They deserve your attention and care, even if all you do is smile and say hello."

I've never forgotten that important lesson. Everyone in my life is important: my family, friends, colleagues and every student. By the way, I also learned her name was Dorothy.

1. **Attitude of Gratitude:** Write the name of one person and something you are grateful for today:

   ____

2. Write the name (or initials) of one person you will listen to and encourage today:

   ____

Day Three

Today's Date: ____________________

Positive Affirmation Thought for the Day: (Write on an index card and carry with you.)

**"In life, I will find exactly what I look for.
I will look for the best in people today!"**

Lighter Side of Teaching:

"Teachers Get Paid Too Much"

I am fed up with teachers and their hefty salary guides. What we need here is a little perspective. If I had my way, I'd pay teachers myself, and I would pay them baby sitting wages. That's right – instead of paying these outrageous taxes I'd give teachers $3 an hour out of my own pocket. Also, I would only pay them for 5 hours a day, not for coffee breaks. That would be $15 a day. Now, if each parent paid them $15, even if they have more than one child in school, it would still be cheaper than paying for private day care.

If each teacher has 25 students, that would be 25 x $15 = $375 a day. But remember, they only work 180 days per year. I am not going to pay them for all those vacations! So, $375 x 180 = $67,500. (Just a minute, I think my calculator needs batteries.) Now I know you teachers will say, "What about those who have 10 years experience and a Master's Degree?" Well, maybe to be fair, they could get the minimum wage, and instead of just baby sitting, they could read the children a story.

We can round that off to about $5 an hour, 5 hours a day, times 25 students, equals $625 a day x 180 days = $112,500 a year . . . Wait a minute! Let's get a little perspective here. Baby sitting wages are obviously too good for these teachers. Did anyone see a salary guide around here?

Author Unknown (could not be found)

Inspiration/Motivation:

"The Dash"

I read of a man who stood to speak, at the funeral of his friend;
He referred to the dates on her tombstone, from the beginning . . . to the end.
He noted that first came her date of birth, he spoke of the second with tears;
But he said what mattered most of all, was the "dash" between the years.

For that little "dash" represents all the time, she spent alive on earth;

And now only those who loved her, know what that little "dash" is worth.
For it matters not how much we own, the cars, the house, the cash;
What matters is how we live and love, and how we spend our "dash";

So, think about this long and hard, are there things you need to change? You never know how much time is left, you could be at "dash mid-range." If we could slow down long enough, to consider what's true and real. And always try to understand, the way other people feel.

And . . . be less quick to anger, and show appreciation more;
And love the people in our lives, like we've never loved before.
If we treat each other with respect, and more often wear a smile;
Remembering that their special "dash", might only last a little while.

So, when your eulogy is read, with your life's actions to rehash;
Will you be pleased with the things they say,
About how you spent your "dash"?

1. **Attitude of Gratitude:** Write the name of one person and something you are grateful for today:

   ____

2. Write the name (or initials) of one person you will listen to and encourage today:

   ____

Day Four

Today's Date: ___________________

Positive Affirmation Thought for the Day: (Write on an index card and carry with you.)

"I will <u>get</u> students' best effort only when I <u>expect</u> their best effort!"

<u>Lighter Side of Teaching</u>:

"There's an Excuse, and School's Get Most of 'Em"
(Spelling and grammar exactly as submitted to teachers)

- Dear School: Please ackuse John for being absent on Jan. 29, 30, 31, 32, 33
- Chris has an acre in his side
- Jim has been absent because he had two teeth taken off his face
- I kept Billie home because she had to go Christmas shopping because I didn't know what size she wear
- Please excuse Gloria. She has been sick and under the doctor
- My son is under the doctor's care and should not take P.E. Please execute him
- Please excuse Ray Friday. He had loose vowels

- Please excuse Blanche from jim today. She is administrating
- Please excuse Jamie from being. It was his father's fault
- Maryann was absent December 11-16, because she had a fever, sore throat, headache, and upset stomach. Her sister was also sick, fever and sore throat and ached all over. I wasn't the best either, sore throat and fever. There must be the flu going around, her father even got hot last night

Inspiration/Motivation:

"The Father's Eyes"

This teenager lived alone with his father, and the two of them had a very special relationship. Even though the son was always on the bench, his father was always in the stands cheering. He never missed a game. This young man was the smallest of the class when he entered high school. His father continued to encourage him but also made it very clear that he did not have to play football if he didn't want to. But the young man loved football and decided to hang in there. He was determined to try his best at every practice, and perhaps he'd get to play when he became a senior.

All through high school he never missed a practice nor a game, but remained a bench warmer all four years. His faithful father was always in the stands, always with words of encouragement for him. When the young man went to college, he decided to try out for the football team as a "walk-on." Everyone was sure he wouldn't make the cut, but he did. The coach admitted that he kept him on the roster because he always put his heart and soul into every practice, and at the same time provided the other members with the spirit and hustle they badly needed.

The news that he had survived the cut thrilled him so much that he rushed to the nearest phone and called his father. His father shared his excitement and was sent season tickets for all the college games. The persistent young man never missed practice during his four years at college, but he never got to play in a game. It was the end of his senior football season, an as he trotted onto the practice field shortly before the big playoff game, the coach met him with a telegram. The young man read the telegram and he became deathly silent. Swallowing hard, he mumbled to the coach, "My father died this morning. Is it all right if I miss practice today?" The coach put his arm gently around his shoulder and said, "Take the rest of the week off, son. And don't even worry about coming back to the game on Saturday."

Saturday arrived, and the game was not going well. In the third quarter, when the team was ten points behind, a silent young man quietly slipped into the empty locker room and put on his football gear. As he ran onto the sidelines, the coach and his players were astounded to see their faithful teammate back so soon. "Coach, please let me play. I've just got to play today," said the young man. The coach pretended not to hear him. There was no way he was going to play the worst player on the team in this close playoff game. But the young man persisted, and finally feeling sorry for the kid, the coach gave in. "All right, you can go in."

Before long, the coach, the players and everyone in the stands could not believe their eyes. This little unknown, who had never played before was doing everything right. The opposing team could not stop him. He tackled like a star. Because of his spirit and intensity, his team began to improve. The score was soon tied. In the closing seconds of the game, this kid intercepted a pass and ran all the way for the winning touchdown. The fans broke loose. His teammates hoisted him onto their shoulders. Such cheering you've never heard.

Finally, after the stands had emptied and the team had showered and left the locker room, the coach noticed that the young man was sitting quietly in the corner all alone. The coach walked over to him and said, "Kid, I can't believe it. You were fantastic! Tell me what got in to you. How did you do it?"

He looked at the coach, with tears in his eyes, and said, "Well, you know my dad died, but did you know that my dad was blind?" The young man swallowed hard and forced a smile, "Dad came to all my games, but today was the first time he could see me play, and I wanted to show him I could do it!"

1. **Attitude of Gratitude:** Write the name of one person and something you are grateful for today:

   ____

2. Write the name (or initials) of one person you will listen to and encourage today.

   ____

Day Five

Today's Date: ____________________

Positive Affirmation Thought for the Day: (Write on an index card and carry with you.)

"Someone's <u>opinion</u> of me does not have to become my <u>reality</u>!"

(There is a BIG difference between opinions and reality.)

<u>Lighter Side of Teaching</u>:

"Teachers Didn't Larn 'Em Much"

(The following were actual answers to a 6th grade history test.)

1. Ancient Egypt was inhabited by mummies and they all wrote in hydraulics. They lived in Sarah's Dessert. The climate of the Sarah is such that the inhabitants have to live elsewhere.

2. The Greeks were a highly sculptured people, and without them we wouldn't have history. The Greeks also had myths. A myth is a female moth.

3. Socrates was a famous Greek teacher who went around giving people advice. They killed him. Socrates died from an overdose of wedlock. After his death, his career suffered a dramatic decline.
4. In the Olympic games, Greeks ran races, jumped, hurled biscuits, and threw the Java.
5. Joan of Arc was burnt to a steak and was canonized by Bernard Shaw
6. The greatest writer of the Renaissance was William Shakespeare. He was born in the year 1564, supposedly on his birthday. He wrote tragedies, comedies, and hysterectomies, all in Islamic pentameter.
7. On April 14, 1865, Lincoln went to the theater and got shot in his seat by one of the actors in a moving picture show. They believe that the assassinator was John Wilkes Booth, a supposingly insane actor. This ruined Booth's career.
8. Handel, the famous composer, was half German, half Italian and half English. He was very large.
9. The nineteenth century was a time of great inventions. People started reproducing by machine. Cyrus McCormick invented the McCormick raper, which did the work of a hundred men. During this time Karl Marx became one of the Marx brothers.

Inspiration/Motivation:

"The Character of a Highly Successful Teacher"

Standing for what you believe in, regardless of the odds against you;
And the pressure that tears at your resistance, . . . means *courage*!

Keeping a smile on your face, when inside you feel like dying;
For the sake of supporting others . . . means *strength*!

Stopping at nothing, and doing what's in your heart;
You know is right . . . means *determination*!

Doing more than is expected, to make another's life a little more bearable;
Without uttering a single complaint . . . means *compassion*!

Helping someone in need, no matter the time or effort;
To the best of your ability . . . means *loyalty*!

Giving more than you have, and expecting nothing;
Absolutely nothing in return . . . means *selflessness*!

Holding your head high, and being the best you know you can be,
When life seems to fall apart at your feet;
Facing each difficulty with the confidence, that time will bring you better tomorrows;
And never, never, never, never giving up . . . means *confidence*!

Author Unknown

1. Write the name of one person and something you are grateful for today:

   ____

2. Write the name (or initials) of one person you will listen to and encourage today.

   ____

Day Six

Today's Date: ________________________

Positive Affirmation Thought for the Day: (Write on an index card and carry with you.)

"I will not let the things I cannot do interrupt the things I can do!"

Lighter Side of Teaching:

"Could You Be An Elementary Teacher?"

- Do you ask guests if they remembered their scarves and mittens as they leave your home?

- Do you move your dinner partner's glass away from the edge of the table?
- When you go to the movie with a group of friends, do you ask for a show of hands from everyone who needs to go the bathroom?
- When a shopper squeezes in front of you in a checkout line, do you tell him/her, "We don't allow cutting in line, so I think you need to go see the principal about this?"
- Do you say everything twice? I mean, do you repeat everything?
- Do you fold your spouse's fingers over the coins as you hand him/her change?
- Do you say, "I like the way you did that" to the mechanic who repaired your car?
- Do you ask a quiet person at a party if s/he has something to share with the group?

Inspiration/Motivation:

"Food for Teacher's Thoughts"

I've learned . . . that it's not *what* you have in your life that counts, but *who* you have in your life that counts.
I've learned . . . that you shouldn't compare yourself with the best others can do.
I've learned . . . that it is taking me a long time to become the person I want to be.

I've learned . . . that you can keep going long after you think you can't.

I've learned . . . that I *can* control my attitude.

I've learned . . . that sometimes the people you expect to kick you when you're down will be the ones who help you get back up.

I've learned . . . that just because someone doesn't love you the way you want them to, doesn't mean they don't love you with all they have.

I've learned . . . that no matter how good a friend is, they're going to hurt you every once in awhile, and you must forgive them for that.

I've learned . . . that our background and circumstances may have influenced who we are, but *we* are responsible for who we become.

I've learned . . . that even when you think you have no more to give, when someone cries out to you, you will find the strength to help.

I've learned . . . that teachers should *never* tell a student their dreams are stupid or unattainable. Few things are more humiliating, and what a tragedy it would be if they believed it. People who don't have dreams don't have very much.

I've learned . . . that the people you care about most in life, you sometimes treat the worst and they are taken from you too soon. **You need to treat everyone the way you would like to be treated, every day . . . beginning today!**

Note: Before completing the 2 questions below, review your answers from Days 1-5. Continue to be grateful for those already listed and continue to listen to and encourage those you thought of previously.

1. Write the name of one person and something you are grateful for today:

   ____

2. Write the name (or initials) of one person you will listen to and encourage today:

   ____

Day Seven

Today's Date: _______________

Positive Affirmation Thought for the Day: (Write on an index card and carry with you.)

"People will know how much I care by how well I listen to them."

Lighter Side of Teaching:

"Politically Correct School"

- No one failed your class. They're merely "passing impaired."
- You don't put students in detention. You assign an "exit delay."
- It's not called teacher-lounge-gossip. It's "the speedy transmission of near-factual information."
- Students aren't lazy. They are just "energetically declined."
- Students don't sleep in class. They are "rationing consciousness."
- You are not late for work. You have a "rescheduled arrival time."
- Students don't talk too much in class. They're just "abundantly verbal."
- The food in the school cafeteria isn't awful. It's "digestively challenged."
- You're not having a bad hair day. You're suffering from "rebellious follicle syndrome."

Motivation/Inspiration:

"One Person Can Change A Life"

One day, when I was a freshman in high school, I saw a kid from my class walking home from school. His name was Kurt. It looked like he was carrying all of his books. I thought to myself, "Why would anyone bring home all his books on a Friday? He must really be a nerd." I had quite a weekend planned (parties and a football game tomorrow night), so I shrugged my shoulders and went on.

As I was walking, I saw a bunch of kids running toward him. They ran at him, knocking all his books out of his arms and tripping him so he landed in the dirt. His glasses went flying, and I saw them land in the grass about 10 feet from him. He looked up and I saw this terrible sadness in his eyes. My heart went out to him. So, I jogged over to him and as he crawled around looking for his glasses, I saw tears in his eyes.

As I handed him his glasses, I said, "Those guys are jerks. They really should get lives." He looked at me and said, "Hey thanks!" There was a big smile on his face. It was one of those smiles that showed real gratitude. I helped him pick up his books, and asked him where he lived. As it turned out, he lived near me, so I asked him why I had never seen him before. He said he had gone to a private school before now. I had never hung out with a private school kid before. We talked all the way home, and

I carried his books. He turned out to be a pretty cool kid. I asked him if he wanted to play football on Saturday with me and my friends. He said, "Yes." We hung out together all weekend and the more we got to know Kurt, the more we liked him.

Monday morning came, and there was Kurt with the huge stack of books again. I stopped him and said, "You're gonna build some serious muscles carrying that huge pile of books every day!" He just laughed and handed me half the books. Over the next four years, Kurt and I became best friends. When we were seniors, we began to think about college. I knew that we would always be friends, that the miles would never be a problem. He was going to be a doctor and I was going for business and a football scholarship. Kurt was valedictorian of our class. I teased him all the time about being a nerd. He had to prepare a speech for graduation. I was so glad it wasn't me having to get up there and speak.

Graduation day, I saw Kurt. He looked great. He was one of those guys that really found himself during high school. He had more dates than me and all the girls loved him. But, I could see that he was nervous about his speech. So, I smacked him on the back and said, "Hey, you'll be great!" He looked at me with one of those really grateful looks and smiled. "Thanks," he said. A few minutes later, he approached the podium, cleared his throat, and began.

"Graduation is a time to thank those who helped you make it through those tough years. Your parents, your teachers, your siblings, maybe a coach . . . but mostly your friends. I am here to tell all of you that being a friend to someone is the best gift you can give them. I am going to tell you a story."

I just looked at my friend with disbelief as he told the story of the first day we met. He shared how the day I helped him pick up his books, he was planning to kill himself over the weekend. He talked of how he had cleaned out his locker, so his mom wouldn't have to do it later. He looked hard at me and gave me a little smile. "Thankfully, I was saved. My friend saved me from doing the unspeakable."

I heard gasps go through the crowd as this popular student told us all about his weakest moment. I saw his Mom and dad looking at me and smiling that same grateful smile. Not until that moment did I realize it's depth.

Never underestimate the power of your words and actions. You can change someone's life every day. Why not start today?

1. **Attitude of Gratitude:** Write the name of one person and something you are grateful for today:____________

2. Write the name (or initials) of one person you will listen to and encourage today: ____________________

Day Eight

Today's Date: ________________

Positive Affirmation Thought for the Day: (Write on an index card and carry with you.)

"Life is 10% what happens to me and 90% what I do about it!"

Lighter Side of Teaching:

"Students Are Smarter Than We Think"

(Elementary students were asked to complete the following adult "words of wisdom.")

- Better to be safe than . . . punch a 5th grader.
- Strike while the . . . bug is close.
- It's always darkest before . . . daylight savings time.
- Never underestimate the power of . . . termites.
- Don't bite the hand that . . . looks dirty.
- A miss is as good as a . . . Mister.

- You can't teach an old dog . . . new math.
- The pen is mightier than the . . . pigs.
- An idle mind is . . . the best way to relax.
- A penny saved is . . . not much.
- Don't put off tomorrow what . . . you put on to go to bed.
- If at first you don't succeed . . . get new batteries.
- When the blind lead the blind . . . get out of the way.
- There's no fool like . . . Uncle Eddie.

Inspiration/Motivation:

"Things I Think I Own"

Today I stood at my window and cursed the pouring rain,
Today a desperate farmer prayed for his fields of grain.
My weekend plans are ruined, it almost makes me cry,
While the farmer lifts his arms and blesses the clouded sky.

The alarm went off on Monday and I cursed my job routine,
Next door a laid-off worker, feels the empty pockets of his jeans.
I can't wait for my vacation, some time to take for me,
He doesn't know tonight, how he'll feed his family.

I cursed my leaky roof and the grass I need to mow,

A homeless man downtown, checks for change in the telephone.
I need a new car, mine is getting really old,
He huddles in a doorway, seeking shelter from the cold.

With blessings I'm surrounded – the rain, a job, a home,
Though my eyes are often blinded by the things I *think* I own.

1. **Attitude of Gratitude**: Write the name of one person and something you are grateful for today:

   ____

2. Write the name (or initials) of one person you will listen to and encourage today:

   ____

Day Nine

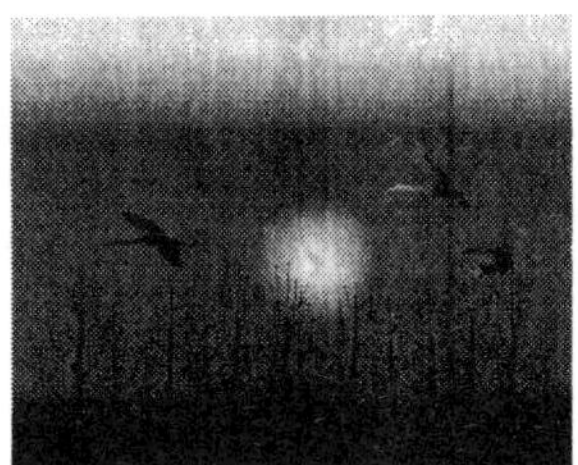

Today's Date:_____________

Positive Affirmation Thought for the Day: (Write on an index card and carry with you.)

"Only one thing will determine what kind of day I have today –my ATTITUDE! I <u>will</u> have a great day!"

<u>Lighter Side of Teaching</u>:

"Things Teachers Learned from Kids At Home"

- When you hear the toilet flush and hear the words, "Uh-oh," it's already too late.
- Certain Legos will pass through the digestive tract of a four-year-old.
- Play Dough and microwave should never be used in the same sentence.
- Super Glue really is "forever."
- VCR's do not eject PB&J sandwiches even though TV commercials show they do.
- Garbage bags do not make good parachutes.
- Marbles in gas tanks make a lot of noise when driving.

- Always look in the oven before you turn it on. Plastic toys do not like ovens.
- The spin cycle on the washing machine does not make earth worms dizzy. It will, however, make cats dizzy, and cats throw up twice their body weight when dizzy.

Teacher Inspiration/Motivation:

"Too Busy for Others"

A teacher came home from school, late in the evening – again – tired and irritated after a long day in the classroom, to find his 5-year old son waiting for him at the door. "Daddy, may I ask you a question?" "Yeah, what is it?" replied the teacher. "Daddy, how much money do you make an hour?" "That's none of your business. What makes you ask such a thing?" the teacher said angrily. "I just want to know. Please tell me, how much do you make an hour?" pleaded his little boy. "First, I don't get paid by the hour, but I guess if you added all the time I spend in after-school meetings, grading papers, and on field trips, if you have to know, I probably make about $15.00 per hour."

"Oh," his little boy replied, head bowed. Looking up, he said, "Daddy, may I borrow $10.00 please?" The father was furious. "If the only reason you wanted to know how much I make is just so you can borrow some to buy a silly toy or some other nonsense, then you march yourself straight to your room and go to bed. Think about why you're being so selfish. I work long, hard hours ever day and don't have time for such childish games."

The little boy quietly went to his room and shut the door. His dad sat down and started to get even madder about the little boy's questioning. How dare he ask such questions only to get some money. After an hour or so, the man had calmed down, and started to think he may have been a little hard on his son. Maybe there was something he really needed to buy with that $10.00. And he really didn't ask for money very often.

He went to his son's room and opened the door. "Are you asleep son?" he asked. "No, Daddy, I'm awake," replied the boy. "I've been thinking, maybe I was too hard on you earlier," he said. "It's been a long day at school and I took my aggravation out on you. Here's that $10.00 you asked for."

His son sat straight up, beaming. "Oh, thank you daddy" he yelled. Then, reaching under his pillow, he pulled out five crumpled one-dollar bills. His dad, seeing that his son already had money, started to get angry again. The little boy slowly counted out his money, then looked up at his dad.

"Why did you want more money if you already had some?" his father grumbled. Because I didn't have enough, but now I do," his son replied. Handing the $15.00 to his dad, he asked, "Daddy, now I have $15.00. Can I have one hour of your time?"

1. **Attitude of Gratitude:** Write the name of one person and something you are grateful for today:

   ____

2. Write the name (or initials) of one person you will listen to and encourage today:

   ____

Day Ten

Today's Date: ______________________

Positive Affirmation Thought for the Day: (Write on an index card and carry with you.)

"Today I will be a <u>dream maker</u> ,
not a <u>dream breaker</u>!"

<u>Lighter Side of Teaching</u>:

(Note: To help put life in perspective, "*Attending College*" may not be everyone's goal in life.)

<u>Things I Wish Teachers Had Taught Me!</u>

No one is ever completely prepared for what college brings. I was entering my first year in college, and I knew there would be differences in the way my life would change. However, when preparing for college I believe teachers should develop a curriculum for graduating seniors in high school that gives them an idea of the insaneness they are about to embark on as a college freshmen. A class that shows how to use your last $2 for a 3 a.m. pizza run. Or maybe on the first day they could move all your belongings into a 10 x 12 box with another person and let you call it "home" for awhile.

Another effective task would be to teach students the proper techniques and times to ask for money from your parents. (This one could be a course by itself.) You could learn the typical "Road Trip" tips, and be placed in situations only a college student could ever get into. (Ex: You are 5 hours from school with no money, your car just broke down, you haven't showered in 3 days, and you're starved because you haven't eaten since the pizza at the concert last night...what do you do hot shot?!) There could also be a separate class deemed "Pranks 101" where you learn the basics of not only how to act when you are on the receiving end of a prank, but how to make sure it never happens again. (Ex: A tipped trash can filled with water and sour milk under their door at 2 in the morning.)

A typical class could consist of everyone taking a nap and then someone pulling the fire alarm so that everyone has to go stand in 30 degrees below freezing weather with nothing but your underwear and sandals on for half an hour. When all is said and done, nothing would really help the high school student prepare for college any more than learning the magnificent art that will become the product and the solution to all their problems....**Procrastination!**

by Jon King

"College Application Essay"

INSTRUCTIONS: In order for the admissions staff of our college to get to know you, the applicant, better, we ask that you answer the following question:

Are there any significant experiences you have had, or accomplishments you have realized, that have helped to define you as a person? (In other words, "have you attended college" since high school? If not, what specific talents or abilities, (if any), do you possess?)

I am a dynamic figure, often seen scaling walls and crushing ice. I have been known to remodel train stations on my lunch breaks, making them more efficient in the area of heat retention. I translate ethnic slurs for Cuban refugees. I write award-winning operas. I manage time efficiently. Occasionally, I tread water for three days in a row.

I woo women with my sensuous trombone playing. I can pilot bicycles up severe inclines with unflagging speed, and I cook Thirty-Minute Brownies in twenty minutes. Using only a hoe and a large glass of water, I once single-handedly defended a small village in the Amazon Basin from a horde of ferocious army ants. I play bluegrass cello. I was scouted by the Yankees. I am the subject of numerous documentaries. When I'm bored, I build large suspension bridges in my yard. I enjoy urban hang-gliding. On Wednesdays, after school, I repair electrical appliances free of charge.

I am an abstract artist and a concrete analyst. Critics world-wide swoon over my original line of corduroy evening wear. I don't perspire. I am a private citizen, yet I receive fan mail. I have been caller number nine and have won the weekend passes. Last summer I toured New Jersey with a traveling centrifugal-force demonstration. I bat 400. My deft floral arrangements have earned me fame in international botany circles. Children trust me.

I can hurl tennis rackets at small moving objects with deadly accuracy. I once read *Paradise Lost, Moby Dick,* and *David Copperfield* in one day and still had time to refurbish an entire dining room that evening. I know the exact location of every food item in the supermarket. I have performed several covert operations for the CIA. I sleep once a week; when I do sleep, I sleep in a chair. While on vacation in Canada, I successfully negotiated with a group of terrorists who had seized a small bakery. The laws of physics do not apply to me.

I balance, I weave, I dodge, I frolic, and my bills are all paid. I have made extraordinary four-course meals using only a bowl and a toaster oven. I breed prize-winning clams. I have won bullfights in San Juan, cliff-diving competitions in Sri Lanka, and spelling bees at the Kremlin. I have played Hamlet, I have performed open-heart surgery, and I have spoken with Elvis.

But . . . I am sorry to say . . . **I have not yet <u>attended college</u>!!**

Teacher Inspiration/Motivation:

(IMPORTANT: If you have previously read this, please take the time to read it again. It is one of the most powerful pieces I've ever seen for teachers. Notice the dramatic difference it makes when the teacher in this true story eventually practices *The 6 Dynamic Strategies of Highly Successful Teachers* . . . caring attitude, high expectations, connecting personally with the student etc.)

"3 Letters From Teddy"

Teddy's letter came today, and now that I've read it, I will place it in my cedar chest with the other things that are important in my life. "I wanted you to be the first to know." I smiled as I read the words he had written and my heart swelled with a pride that I had no right to feel. I have not seen Teddy Stallard since he was a student in my 5th grade class, 15 years ago. It was early in my career, and I had only been teaching two years.

From the first day he stepped into my classroom, I disliked Teddy. Teachers (although everyone knows differently) are not supposed to have favorites in a class, but most especially are not supposed to show dislike for a child, any child. Nevertheless, every year there are one or two children that one cannot help but be attached to, for teachers are human, and it is human nature to like bright, pretty, intelligent people, whether they are 10 years old or 25. And sometimes, not too often, fortunately, there will be one or two students to whom the teacher just can't seem to relate.

I had thought myself quite capable of handling my personal feelings along that line until Teddy walked into my life. There wasn't a child I particularly liked that year, but Teddy was most assuredly one I disliked. He was dirty. Not just occasionally, but all the time. His hair hung low over his ears, and he actually had to hold it out of his eyes as he wrote his papers in class. (And this was before it was fashionable to do so!)

His physical faults were many, and his intellect left a lot to be desired, also. By the end of the first week I knew he was hopelessly behind the others. Not only was he behind; he was just plain slow! I began to withdraw from him immediately.

Any teacher will tell you that it's more of a pleasure to teach a bright child. It is definitely more rewarding for one's ego. But any teacher worth her credentials can channel work to the bright child, keeping him challenged and learning, while she puts her major effort on the slower ones. Any teacher can do this. Most teachers do it, but I didn't, not that year.

In fact, I concentrated on my best students and let the others follow along as best they could. Ashamed as I am to admit it, I took perverse pleasure in using my red pen; and each time I came to Teddy's papers, the cross marks (and they were many) were always a little larger and a little redder than necessary. "Poor work!" I would write with a flourish.

While I did not actually ridicule the boy, my attitude was obviously quite apparent to the class, for he quickly became the class "goat", the outcast – the unlovable and the unloved. He knew I didn't like him, but he didn't know why. Nor did I know – then or now – why I felt such an intense dislike for him. All I

The days rolled by. We made it through the Fall Festival and the Thanksgiving holidays, and I continued marking happily with my red pen. As the Christmas holidays approached, I knew that Teddy would never catch up in time to be promoted to the sixth grade level. He would be a repeater. To justify myself, I went to his cumulative folder from time to time. He had very low grades for the first four years, but had not failed a grade. How he had made it, I didn't know. I closed my mind to personal remarks I read.

First grade: Teddy shows promise by work and attitude, but has poor home situation. Second grade: Teddy could do better. Mother terminally ill. He receives little help at home. Third grade: Teddy is a pleasant boy. Helpful, but too serious. Slow learner. Mother passed away at end of year. Fourth grade: Very slow, but well-behaved. Father shows no interest.

Well, they passed him four times, but he will certainly repeat fifth grade! "Do him good!" I said to myself. And then the last day before the holiday arrived. Our little tree on the reading table sported paper and popcorn chains. Many gifts were heaped underneath, waiting for the big moment. Teachers always get several gifts at Christmas, but mine that year seemed bigger and more elaborate than ever. There was not a student who had not brought me one. Each unwrapping brought squeals of delight, and the proud giver would receive effusive thank-you's.

His gift wasn't the last one I picked up; in fact it was in the middle of the pile. Its wrapping was a brown paper bag, and he had colored Christmas trees and red bells all over it. It was stuck together with masking tape. "For Mrs. Thompson – From Teddy" it read. The group was completely silent, and for the first time, I felt conspicuous, embarrassed because they all stood watching me unwrap that gift.

As I removed the last bit of masking tape, two items fell to my desk; a gaudy rhinestone bracelet with several stones missing and a small bottle of dime store cologne – half empty. I could hear the snickers and whispers, and I wasn't sure I could look at Teddy. "Isn't this lovely?" I asked, placing the bracelet on my wrist. "Teddy, would you help me fasten it?" He smiled shyly as he fixed the clasp, and I held up my wrist for all of them to admire. There were a few hesitant oohs and aahs, and as I dabbed the cologne behind my ears, all the little girls lined up for a dab behind their ears.

I continued to open the gifts until I reached the bottom of the pile. We ate our refreshments and the bell rang. The children filed out with shouts of "See you next year!" and "Merry Christmas!" but Teddy waited at his desk. When they had all left, he walked toward me, clutching his books to his chest.

"You smell just like Mom," he said softly. "Her bracelet looks real pretty on you, too. I'm glad you liked it." He left quickly. I locked the door, sat down at my desk, and wept, resolving to make up to Teddy what I had deliberately deprived him of – **a teacher who cared**.

I stayed every afternoon with Teddy from the end of the Christmas holidays until the last day of school. Sometimes we worked together. Sometimes he worked alone while I drew up lesson plans or graded papers. Slowly but surely he caught up with the rest of the class. Gradually, there was a definite upward curve in his grades.

He did not have to repeat the 5th grade. In fact, his final averages were among the highest in the class, and although I knew he would be moving out of the state when school was out, I was not worried for him. Teddy had reached a level that would stand him in good stead the following year, no matter where he went. He enjoyed a measure of success, and as we were taught in our teacher training courses, "Success builds success."

I did not hear from Teddy until seven years later, when his first letter appeared in my mailbox:

Dear Miss Thompson,
"I just wanted you to be the first to know. I will be graduating second in my class next month."
Very Truly Yours,
Teddy Stallard

I sent him a card of congratulations and a small package, a pen and pencil gift set. I wondered what he would do after graduation.

Four years later Teddy's second letter came:

Dear Miss Thompson,
" I wanted you to be the first to know. I was just informed that I'll be graduating first in my class. The university has not been easy, but I liked it."
Very Truly Yours,
Teddy Stallard

I sent him a good pair of sterling silver monogrammed cuff links and a card, so proud of him I could burst!

And now today – Teddy's third letter:

Dear Miss Thompson,
" I wanted you to be the first to know. As of today, I am Theodore J. Stallard, M. D. How about that? I am going to be married in July, the 27th to be exact. I wanted to ask if you could come and sit where Mom would sit if she were still here. I'll have no family there as Dad died last year."
Very Truly Yours,
Teddy Stollard

I'm not sure what kind of gift one sends to a doctor on completion of medical school and state boards. Maybe I'll just wait and take a wedding gift, but my note can't wait:

Dear Teddy,
"Congratulations! You made it, and you did it yourself! In spite of those like me and not because of us, this day has come to you. God bless you. I'll be at that wedding with bells on!"
Elizabeth Silance Ballard

1. Review your previous items listed in Days 1-9 and write the names of the people and things you are **most thankful for**:

2. Write the names (or initials) of two "Teddy Stallards" you have in your class whom you will make a commitment to "connect and care for" the rest of the year – even though you may not want to.

___

IMPORTANT NOTE:

Continue your *"Personal Power Plan of Action"* every day. Look for inspirational resources (either from the suggested list or your own) and have them easily available to read or listen to each morning before you begin your daily teaching responsibilities.

Suggestion: Along with your reading/listening, complete a Daily Log Book. Simply take a minute to record things such as: one humorous thing that happened yesterday, one hard-to-reach student I gave an extra effort to yesterday, one thing I am grateful for etc. Be creative and think of your own personal categories. Have these resources in an easy-to-find place. If you have to "look for it" each morning, unexpected things will happen and it will be difficult to have your "daily quiet time." Make a personal commitment that "no matter what happens" you will make time to mentally prepare yourself for the day. Have an awesome day – every day!

References & Recommendations

Someone once said, "There are no 'original' thoughts recorded in any book. Everything that is written has already been thought of by someone else."

I don't know if that statement is true, but I do know every effort has been made to give credit to and recognize individuals whose work contributed to this book. Any omission of a person's name or title of their work is completely unintentional. I provide the following list not only with appreciation for their thoughts and hard work, but also to recommend that you support their efforts by investing in the purchase of their literary research and/or publication.

1. *The Winning Attitude*, John C. Maxwell, (Thomas Nelson, 1993)
2. *Live Your Dreams*, Les Brown, (William Morrow Co., 1992)
3. *Your Child's Self-Esteem*, Dorothy C. Griggs, (Doubleday, 1970)
4. *Chicken Soup for the Soul*, Jack Canfield and Mark Hansen, (Health Communications, 1993)
5. *Awaken the Giant Within*, Anthony Robbins, (Fireside, 1991)

6. *Positive Personality Profiles*, Robert A. Rohm, (Personality Insights, 1992)
7. *Different Children Different Needs*, David Boehi and Robert A. Rohm, (Questar Publishers, 1994)
8. *The First Days of School*, Harry K. and Rosemary T. Wong, (Harry Wong Publications, 1998)
9. *The Accelerated Learning Handbook*, Dave Meir, (McGraw-Hill, 2000)
10. *Teachers Attribute*, Armand Eisen, (Andrews and McMeel, 1996)
11. *Teacher, A Little Book of Appreciation*, Jesse Hartland, (Running Press, 1999)
12. *Erasing My Sanity!*, Kimberly Chambers, (Great Quotations Publishing Co., 2000)
13. *Teacher's Little Book of Wisdom*, Bob Algozzine, (ICS Books, 1995)
14. *A Teacher is a Special Person!*, Dr. Bernard E. Farber, (Peter Pauper Press, 1996)

Teaching...Take This Job and Love It!

You Can Schedule Jerry King...

for an Exciting In-Service Presentation in Your School Division or An Inspirational Keynote Speaker at Your Next Teacher Conference!

"We had to move Jerry's presentation at our teacher conference to a large ballroom at the Opryland Hotel in Nashville because over 500 teachers attended! He is an exciting, spellbinding and inspiring speaker who knows how to connect with teachers!"

B. Mont Bush,
Southern Assoc. of College & Schools (SACS)

"As you know, over 700 solemn teachers awaited you for a REQUIRED in-service. The resounding standing ovation that followed your fantastic presentation was indicative of your ability to inspire teachers. What a memorable way to enter the last 25 days of the school year - rejuvenated and ready for the final countdown!"

Pat Climer,
Supervisor of Instruction

Limited Dates Available - CALL TODAY!
FREE Speaker Info. Packet
Kreative Kommunications
1-800-528-5559
jking@tcia.net

PO Box 1139 / 1224 Lynn St.
Hillsville, VA 24343
www.tcia.net/speaker

"Success Notes and Quotes"

Personal Power... your ability to take action!

If You Want Different Results:

Take different action!

Change your game plan!

Success Steps for New Results:

Become a life-long learner

Make a decision - not to accept mediocrity

Take massive action!

It's never too late to become the person you wanted to be.

most important person in your success journey You

most " factor " " " " your self-image!

Do not let someone's opinion of me become my reality!

Stress

Perspective - caused by getting things out of ...

"555" Five days, five months, five years - will it matter?

"Success Notes and Quotes"

Wheel of Life

Physical 7 *

Financial 3

Spiritual 4

Mental 5

Personal 6

Family 1

Career 2

Success begins with an attitude of gratitude!

K S

3 greatest enemies of gratitude

Griping

Complaining

Blaming

"Success Notes and Quotes"